William Page, Henry Joseph Boone Nicholson

St. Alban's Cathedral and Abbey Church

A Guide

PENNSYLVANIA DUTCH.

PENNSYLVANIA DUTCH:

A DIALECT OF SOUTH GERMAN WITH AN

INFUSION OF ENGLISH.

BY

S. S. HALDEMAN, A.M.

PROFESSOR OF COMPARATIVE PHILOLOGY IN THE UNIVERSITY OF PENNSYLVANIA,
PHILADELPHIA.

LONDON:

TRÜBNER & CO., 8 AND 60, PATERNOSTER ROW.

1872.

HERTFORD:
PRINTED BY STEPHEN AUSTIN AND SONS.

NOTICE.

WHILE I was engaged with the third part of my *Early English Pronunciation*, Prof. Haldeman sent me a reprint of some humorous letters by Rauch, entitled *Pennsylvanish Deitsh. De Campain Breefa fum Pit Schwefflebrenner un de Bevvy, si alty, gepublished olly woch in "Father Abraham."* Perceiving at once the analogy between this debased German with English intermixture, and Chaucer's debased Anglo-saxon with Norman intermixture, I requested and obtained such further information as enabled me to give an account of this singular modern reproduction of the manner in which our English language itself was built up, and insert it in the introduction to my chapter on Chaucer's pronunciation, *Early English Pronunciation*, pp. 652-663. But I felt it would be a loss to Philology if this curious living example of a mixture of languages were dismissed with such a cursory notice, and I therefore requested Prof. Haldeman, who by birth and residence, philological and phonetic knowledge, was so well fitted for the task, to draw up a more extended notice, as a paper to be read before the Philological Society of London. Hence arose the following little treatise, of which I, for my own part, can only regret the brevity. But the Philological Society, having recently exhausted most of its resources by undertaking the publication of several extra volumes, was unable to issue another of such length, and hence the present Essay appears independently. Owing to his absence from England and my own connexion with the paper, which I communicated and read to the Philological Society, on 3 June, 1870, Prof.

Haldeman requested me to superintend the printing of his essay, and add anything that might occur to me. This will account for a few footnotes signed with my name. The Professor was fortunately able to examine one revise himself, so, that though I am mainly responsible for the press work, I hope that the errors may be very slight

Sufficient importance does not seem to have been hitherto attached to watching the growth and change of living languages. We have devoted our philological energies to the study of dead tongues which we could not pronounce, and have therefore been compelled to compare by letters rather than by sounds, and which we know only in the form impressed upon them by scholars of various times. The form in which they were originally written is for ever concealed. The form in which they appear in the earliest manuscripts has practically never been published, but has to be painfully collected from a mass of various readings. The form we know is a critical, conjectural form, patched up by men distinguished for scholarship, but for the most part entirely ignorant of the laws which govern the changes of speech. The very orthography is medieval. We are thus enabled to see as little of the real genesis of language, in form, in sound, in grammatical and logical construction, in short in the real pith of philological investigation—the relation of thought to speech-sounds—as the study of a full-grown salmon would enable us to judge of the marvellous development of that beautiful fish. Such studies as the present will, I hope, serve among others to stimulate exertion in the new direction. We cannot learn life by studying fossils alone.

ALEX. J. ELLIS.

KENSINGTON,
23 APRIL, 1872.

William Page, Henry Joseph Boone Nicholson

St. Alban's Cathedral and Abbey Church
A Guide

ISBN/EAN: 9783337007607

Printed in Europe, USA, Canada, Australia, Japan

Cover: Foto ©ninafisch / pixelio.de

More available books at **www.hansebooks.com**

CONTENTS.

PENNSYLVANISCH DEITSCH.

CHAPTER I.

PEOPLE—HISTORY—LOCATION—CONDITION.

The reciprocal influence of languages affords an interesting subject of investigation, and it is the object of this essay to present an outline of a dialect which has been formed within a century, and which continues to be spoken, subject to the influences which developed it. Of such languages, English, Wallachian, and Hindûstânî, are familiar examples. Like other languages, the dialect of German known as Pennsylvania Dutch presents variations due to the limited intercourse of a widely-scattered agricultural population, and to the several dialects brought from abroad, chiefly from the region of the Upper Rhine, and the Neckar, the latter furnishing the Suabian or Rhenish Bavarian element. The language is therefore South German, as brought in by emigrants from Rhenish Bavaria, Baden, Alsace (Alsatia), Würtemberg, German Swisserland, and Darmstadt. There were also natives from other regions, with certain French Neutrals deported from Nova Scotia to various parts of the United States, including the county (Lancaster) where the materials for this essay have been collected. These, and probably some families with French names from Alsace, are indicated by a few proper names, like *Roberdeau, Lebo, Deshong* and *Shunk* (both for *Dejean*), and an occasional word like *júschtaménnt* (in German spelling), the French *justement*, but which a native might take for a condensation of *just-an-dem-ende*.

1

Welsh names like *Jenkins, Evans, Owen, Foulke, Griffith, Morgan,* and *Jones* occur, with the township names of *Brecknock, Caernarvon, Lampeter, Leacock* ('Lea' as *lay*), and in the next county of Chester—*Gwinedd* and *Tredyffrin;* but there seems to have been no fusion between Welsh and German, probably because the Welsh may have spoken English. Local names like *Hanōver, Heidelberg* and *Manheim,* indicate whence some of the early residents came.

The French-American *ville* appears in German Pennsylvania, in *Bechtelville, Engelsville, Greshville, Lederachsville, Scherksville, Schwenksville, Silberlingsville, Wernersville, Zieglerville;* paralleled by the English *town* in *Kutztown, Mertztown, Schäfferstown, Straustown; burg* in *Ickesburg, Landisburg, Rehrersburg;* and the German *dorf* has a representative in *Womelsdorf.*

Pennsylvania German does not occur in the counties along the northern border of the state, but it has extended into Maryland, Western Virginia, Ohio, and farther west; and it has some representatives in western New York, and even in Canada. In many of the cities of the United States, such as Pittsburg, Chicago, Cincinnati, and Saint Louis, recent large accessions from Germany have brought in true German, and to such an extent that the German population of the city of New York is said to exceed that of every European city except Berlin and Vienna. The newer teutonic population differs from the older in living to a great extent in the towns, where they are consumers of beer and tobacco—luxuries to which the older stock and their descendants were and are but little addicted. The numerous allusions to the 'Fatherland' to be met with, belong to the foreign Germans—the natives caring no more for Germany than for other parts of Europe, for they are completely naturalised, notwithstanding their language.

Several thousand Germans had entered Pennsylvania before the year 1689, when a steady stream of emigration set in, and it is stated that their number was 100,000 in 1742, and 280,000 in 1763. They occupied a region which has located the Pennsylvania dialect chiefly to the south-east of the Alleghenies, excluding several counties near Philadelphia. Germantown, six miles from Philadelphia, although settled by Germans, seems to have lost its German character. The language under the name of 'Pennsylvania Dutch' is used by a large part of the country population, and may be constantly heard in the county towns of Easton on the Delaware, Reading (i.e. red-ing) on the Schuylkill, Allentown on the Lehigh, Harrisburg (the State capital) on the Susquehanna, Lebanon, Lancaster, and York.

A fair proportion of the emigrants, including the clergy, were educated, and education has never been neglected among them. The excellent female boarding schools of the Moravians were well supported, not only by the people of the interior, but also by the English-speaking population of the large cities, and of the Southern States—a support which prevented the German accent of some of the teachers from being imitated by the native teutonic pupils—for the education was in English, although German and French were taught. Booksellers find it to their advantage to advertise the current German and English literature in the numerous German journals of the interior, and there is a *Deutsch-Amerikanisches Conversations Lexicon* in course of publication, which gives the following statistics of one of the German counties.

"The German element is strongly and properly represented in Allentown, and in Lehigh county generally, where the German language has retained its greatest purity, and so strong is this element, that in the city itself there are but few persons who speak English exclusively. An evidence of this is found in the fact that in seventy of the eighty Christian congregations in the county, some of which are over one hundred years old, Divine service is conducted in the German language. Allentown has seven German churches: (two Lutheran, one Reformed, two Methodist, one United Brethren, and one Catholic); and nine German journals, of which are published weekly—*Der Unabhängige* [1] *Republikaner* (fifty-nine years old), *Der Friedensbote* (fifty-seven years old), *Der Lecha County Patriot* (forty-three years old), *Der Weltbote* (fifteen years old, with 12,000 subscribers), and *Die Lutherische Zeitschrift*. The *Stadt- und Land-Bote* is a daily, the *Jugendfreund* semi-monthly, with twenty thousand subscribers; and Pastor Brobst's *Theologischen Monatshefte* is monthly. Since the beginning of the year 1869, the German language has been taught in the public schools." [2] The *Reading Adler* is in its seventy-fourth, and the Lancaster *Volksfreund* in its sixty-second year.—Dec. 1869.

¹ Un-ab-häng-ig, un-off-hang-ing, in-de-pend-ent, Polish nie-za-wis-ty.
² Allentown has just completed one of the finest public school buildings in Eastern Pennsylvania.—*Newspaper, February*, 1870.

The convenient quarto German almanacs (with a printed page of about five and a half by seven and a half inches in size), were preferred to the duodecimo English almanacs, even among the non-Germans, until the appearance of English almanacs in the German format about the year 1825. The early settlers were extensive purchasers and occupiers of land, and being thus widely scattered, and having but few good roads, the uniformity of the language is greater than might have been supposed possible. These people seldom became merchants and lawyers, and in the list of attorneys admitted in Lancaster County, commencing with the year 1729, the names are English until 1769, when *Hubley* and *Weitzel* appear. From 1793 to 1804, of fifty-two names, three are German; from 1825 to 1835, twenty-four names give *Reigart* and *Long* (the latter anglicised). After 1860 the proportion is greater, for among the nine attorneys admitted in 1866, we find the German names of *Urich*, *Loop*, *Kauffman*, *Reinœhl*, *Seltzer*, and *Miller*. At the first school I attended as a child, there were but three English family names, and in the playground, English and German games were practised, such as 'blumsak' (G. plumpsack), 'Prisoner's base,' and 'Hink'l-wai[1] was graabscht du do?' which was never played with the colloquy translated.

Pennsylvania Dutch (so called because Germans call themselves *Deutsch*[2]) is known as a dialect which has been corrupted or enriched by English words and idioms under a pure or modified pronunciation, and spoken by natives, some of them knowing no other language, but most of them speaking or understanding English. Many speak both languages vernacularly, with the pure sounds of each, as in distinguishing German *tôd*

---

[1] As if 'bühn-kel weihe' *chicken hawk*, 'wai' rhyming with *boy*.

[2] In an article on (the) "Pennsylvania Dutch" in the 'Atlantic Monthly' (Boston, Mass., Oct., 1869, p. 473), it is asserted that "the tongue which these people speak is not German, nor do they expect you to call it so." On the contrary, the language is strictly a German dialect, as these pages prove. The mistake has arisen from the popular confusion between the terms *Dutch* and *German*, which are synonymous with many. In Albany (New York) they speak of the *Double Dutch Church*, which seems to have been formed by the fusion of a 'German Reformed' with a 'Dutch Reformed' congregation. These are different denominations, now greatly anglicised. In 1867 the Rev. J. C. Dutcher was a Dutch Reformed pastor in New York.

(death) from English *toad;* or English *winter* from German *winter,* with a different *w,* a lengthened *n,* a flat *t,* and a trilled *r*—four distinctions which are natural to my own speech. Children, even when very young, may speak English entirely with their parents, and German with their grandparents, and of two house-painters (father and son) the father always speaks German and the son English, whether speaking together, or with others. The males of a family being more abroad than the females, learn English more readily, and while the father, mother, daughters, and servants may speak German, father and son may speak English together naturally, and not with a view to have two languages, as in Russia. Foreign Germans who go into the interior usually fall into the local dialect in about a year, and one remarked that he did so that he might not be misunderstood. Some of these, after a residence of fifteen or twenty years, speak scarcely a sentence of English, and an itinerant piano-tuner, whose business has during many years taken him over the country, says that he has not found a knowledge of English necessary.

The English who preceded the Germans in Pennsylvania brought their names of objects with them, calling a thrush with a red breast a *robin*; naming a bird not akin to any thrush a *blackbird*; and assigning to a yellow bird the name of *goldfinch,* but adopting a few aboriginal names like *racoon, hackee* and *possum.* The Germans did this to some extent, for *blackbird* saying 'schtaar' (G. *staar,*[1] starling,) for the *goldfinch* (oriole) 'goldamschl,' for the *thrush* (G. *drossel*) 'druschl,' for a *woodpecker* 'specht' (the German name), and for a crow 'krap.'

The *ground-squirrel* is named 'fensemeissli' (fence-mouse-lin, *fence* being English) ; a large grey squirrel is called ' eechhaas' (for *eich-hase,* oak-hare) ; and in Austria a squirrel is akatzel and achkatzel (oak-kitten). The burrowing marmot (Arctomys monax), known as ground-hog, is called 'grun'daks' (from a fancied analogy with the German *dachs* or badger) and

---

[1] Words in single quotations are Pennsylvania German. The system of spelling is described in the next chapter. High German words are commonly in italics, or marked G.

in York County 'grundsau,' a translation of the English name.
The English *patridge* (partridge, Dutch patrijs) is Germanised
into 'pattereesəli' — also called 'feld-hinkli' (little field-
chicken),—hinkl being universally used for *chicken* or *chickens*.

The usual perversions by otōsis occur, as in the city of Baltimore, where foreign Germans say 'Ablass' for *Annapolis*
and 'Kälber Strasze' (Street of Calves) for Calvert Street—but
the citizens themselves have replaced the vowel of *what* with
that of *fat*, in the first syllable of this name; and the people of
New York now pronounce 'Beekman Street' with the syllable *beak* instead of *bake* according to the earlier practice.

A German botanist gave 'Gandoge' as the locality of an
American plant ; a package sent by express to ' Sevaber ' (an
English name), and a letter posted to the town of ' Scur E
Quss, Nu Yourck,' arrived safely ; and I have seen a hand-
board directing the traveller to the English-named town of
'Bintgrof.' As these present no special difficulty, they are
not explained.

English *rickets* for ' rachîtis' is a familiar example of otōsis,
and it appears in the following names of drugs furnished by a
native druggist who speaks both languages, and who was able
to determine the whole from the original prescriptions.

Allaways, Barrickgorrick, Sider in de ment, Essig of Iseck,
Hirim Packer, Cinment, Cienpepper, Sension, Saintcun, Opien,
High cyrap, Seno and mano misct, Sking, Coroces suple-
ment, Red presepeite, Ammeline, Lockwouth, Absom's salts,
Mick nisey, Corgel, Chebubs, By crematarter potash, Balder-
yon, Lower beans, Cots Shyneol.

CHAPTER II.

Phonology of Pennsylvania Dutch.

§ 1. *Use of the Alphabet.*

In his "Key into the Languages of America," London, 1643, Roger Williams says that "the life of all language is pronuntiation"—and in the comparison of dialects it deserves especial attention. To enable the reader the more readily to understand these pages, and to compare the words with literary German, the principles of German orthography will be used as far as they are consistent, but every letter or combination is in every case to be pronounced according to the power here indicated—except in literal quotations, where the originals are followed. A single vowel letter is always to be read short, and when doubled it must have the same sound, but lengthened—but as a single vowel letter is often read long in German, and as short vowels are often indicated by doubling a consonant letter, this absurd mode is sometimes used to prevent mispronunciation through carelessness.[1] The 's' is also sometimes doubled to prevent it from becoming English 'z' with readers who, in careless moods, might rhyme 'as' (as) with *has* instead of *fosse*. In a PG. poem of Rachel Bahn, commencing with—

> "Wie soothing vocal music is!
> Wie herrlich un wie schoe!"

---

[1] For example, as the vowel of German *schaf* is long, the PG. word 'schafleit,' which occurs in a quoted passage farther on, would be likely to be read 'schaafleit' (sheep-people or shepherds) instead of 'schaffleit' (work-people), although it is stated that in the spelling used, a vowel *must not be made long* unless its letter is doubled. "This tendency, and a trick of reading words like nisbut, *relation*, qismut, *fortune*, as if written *nizbut*, *qizmut*, should be carefully guarded against. . . . Even is, as, rusm, will, in spite of the caveat, . . . become again in his mouth iz, az, ruzm, rather than the iss, auss, russm, intended."—*Gilchrist*, 1806.

most English readers would be likely to rhyme 'is' with *phiz* instead of *hiss*, which will be prevented by writing 'iss,' etc.

Although I have visited various counties of the State at distant intervals, the facts given here pertain chiefly to a single locality, so that if it is stated, for example, that 's' with its English sound in 'misery' does not occur, or that 'kəp' (head) is used to the exclusion of *haupt*, it is not intended to assert that such a sound as *z*, or such a word as *haupt*, have not a local existence. In fact, although they are not recorded here, English *z*, *w*, and *v*, may be common enough. A German confounds *met* and *mat*, *cheer* and *jeer*, and when he becomes able to pronounce them all, he not unfrequently creates a new difficulty, and for *cherry* says *järry* (rhyming *carry*), and after he has acquired sounds like English *z*, *w*, and *v*, they might readily slip into his German speech.

The letter *b* and its spirant (German *w*) both occur, and the latter often replaces *b*, in one region 'ich haw' (I have) replaces 'ich hab,' German *ich habe*, and 'nit' replaces 'net' (not), German *nicht*. The vowels of *up* and *ope* interchange, as in 'kəch' or 'koch' (cook) 'nəch' or 'noch' (yet); and it is difficult to determine whether the prefixes *ge-* and *be-* have the vowel of *bet* or *but*. Lastly, the nasal vowels are by some speakers pronounced pure. Should discrepancies be found upon these points, they are to be attributed rather to the dialect than to the writer—or to the two conjointly.

§ 2. *The Vowels.*

E. indicates *English;* G. *German;* SG. *South German;* PG. *Pennsylvania German* (or 'Dutch'); .a preceding dot indicates what would be a capital letter in common print. It is used where capital forms have not been selected, as for æ.

a in what, not; PG. kat (G. gehabt) *had;* kats *cat.*

aa (ah [1]) in fall, orb; PG. haas *hare*; paar *pair*; haan (G. hahn) *cock*; tsaam (G. zaum) *bridle.*

a in aisle, height, out. In a few cases it is written â. See under the dipthongs.

---

[1] High German *letters* which represent PG. *sounds* are in parentheses.

æ (ä, e¹) in fat; hær (G. Herr) *Sir*; dœr (and d'r, G. der) *the*; hærn (G. hirn) *brain*; schtærn, pl. schtærnə (G. stern) *star*; mær (G. mähre) *mare*; œrscht (G. erst) *first*; wærts-haus (G. wirtshaus) *inn*.

œœ (ä, äh) in baa, the preceding vowel lengthened.¹ PG. bœœr (G. bär) *bear*; kæær E. *ear*.

e (ä, ö) in bet; PG. bet *bed*; net (G. nicht) *not*; apnémə (G. abnahme *decline*) PG. a wasting disease; het (G. hätte *had*), which, with some other words, will sometimes be written with ä (hätt) to aid the reader. In a few cases it is lengthened (as in thêre), when it is written ê, as in French.

ee (ä, äh, eh, ö) in ale; PG. meel (G. mehl) *meal*; eel (G. öl) *oil*.

ə (e, o, a) in but, mention;² PG. kəp (G. kopf) *head*; ləs (G. lasz) *let*, hawə (a short, G. haben) *to have*.

i (ü, ie, ö) in finny; niks (G. nichts) *nothing*; tsrik (G. zurück) *back*; miglich (G. möglich) *possible*; lit'rlich (G. liederlich) *riotous*.

ii (ih, ie, ü) in feel; fiil (G. viel) *much*; dii (G. die) *the*; rüwə (G. rübe) *turnip*; wüscht (G. wüst, ü long) *nasty*. It is the French î, which is sometimes used in these pages.

o in o-mit; los *loose*; hofnung *hope*. English o pronounced quickly.

oo in door, home; wool (G. wohl) *well*; groo (G. grau) *grey*.

u in full, foot; mus (G. musz) *must*; fun (G. von) *of*.

uu (uh) in fool; kuu (G. kuh) *cow*; guut (G. gut) *good*.

The true 'a' of arm does not occur, except approximately in the initial of au and ei. The proper sounds of ä, ö, ü are absent, and if these letters are used in a few cases to enable the reader to recognise words, the two former will be restricted to syllables having the vowel sound in *met*, and 'ü' to such as have that in *fit*.

§ 3.   *The Dipthongs.*

ei (eu) in height, aisle, German ei, with the initial '*a*' (italic) of Mr. Ellis (in his *Early English Pronunciation*), 'eu' has the same power in PG.

ai in boy, oil; somewhat rare, but present in the names Boyer, Moyer (from Meyer), ai (G ei) *egg*; ajər (aajər, aijər) *eggs*; hai (G. heu) *hay*; bai (sounding like E. boy, and from E.) *pie*; wai (G. weihe) *hawk*. Literary German has it in 'bäume' *trees*, and 'eu' (which is properly ei) is usually confounded with it in German.

ei, which Mr. Ellis (*ibid.*) gives as the power of English 'ai' (aisle) in London, occurs in the PG. exclamation 'həi,' used in driving cows, and naturalised in the vicinal English. Slavonic has (in German spelling) huj, and Hungarian hü, used in driving swine. Compare Schmidt, Westerwäld. Idiot., p. 276.

¹ The long vowel used by native speakers in Bath, Somersetshire, England.
² These two powers are not quite the same.

au in *house*; G. haus, PG. haus. English 'ou' is thus pronounced in adopted words like 'County,' or 'Caunty,' 'Township' or 'Taunschip.'

Care must be taken not to confound the initial of these pairs, for G. and PG. 'eis' (ice) and 'aus' (out) have the same initial vowel, while 'aistɘr' would spell *oyster*.

§ 4. *Nasal Vowels and Dipthongs.*

PG. is not a harsh dialect, like Swiss. It has, however, the Suabian feature of nasal vowels,[1] but to a less extent. They will be indicated with (ͺ) a modification of the Polish mode. This nasality replaces a lost *n* (but not a lost *m*), and it does not pervert the vowel or dipthong, as in the French *un, vin,* as compared with *une, vinaigre.* Nor does it affect all vowels which have been followed by *n,* for most of them remain pure. Nasal 'ee' (in *they,* French *é*) is very common, but does not occur in French, and French *un* does not occur in PG. Being unaware of the existence of this feature, the writers of the dialect neglect it in the printed examples, which makes it difficult for a foreigner to comprehend them, because a word like 'aa' (the English syllable *awe*) would stand for G. *auch* (also), and when nasal (aaͺ) for G. *an* (on); and 'schtee' would represent both the German *stehe* and *stein,* as in saying 'I stand on the stone'—

G. Ich stehe auf dem stein.—PG. ich schtee uf m schteeͺ.

The following words afford examples :—

aaͺ-fang-ɘ (G. anfangen) *to begin*; alée, (G. allein) *alone*; schee, (G. schön) *handsome*; bee, (G. bein, pl. beine) *leg, legs*; kee, (G. kein) *none*; grii, (G. grün) *green*; duu, (G. thun) *to do.* Was hɘt ær geduu,? (G. Was hat er gethan?) *what has he done?* mei, (G. mein, meine) *my*; dei, (G. dein) *thy*; nei, (G. hinein) *within*; ei, being the only nasal dipthong.

The obscurity arising from a neglect of the nasal vowels appears in the following lines—

"Die amshel singt so huebsch un' feih,
Die lerch sie duht ihr lied ah neih;" . . .
"Awhaemle duht mich eppes noh."—*Rachel Bahn.*

Final *n* is not always rejected; but remains in many words, among which are—'in' *in;* 'bin' *am;* 'un' *and;* 'iin' (him)

---

[1] Indicated in 1860 in my Analytic Orthography, §§ 661-3, and in my note to A. J. Ellis's *Early English Pronunciation,* 1869, p. 655, note 2, col. 2. "The lost final *n* is commonly recalled by a nasal vowel."

G. *ihn* (but hii, for G. *hin* thither); 'fun' (from) G. *von;*
'wan' (when) ; 'hen' (have) G. *haben;* 'kan' (can); 'schun'
(already) G. *schon.*

German infinitives in -en end in -ə in PG., a vowel not subject to nasality, so that when G. *gehen* (to go) remains a dis-
syllable it is 'gee'ə,' but when monosyllabised it becomes 'gee,'
—this vowel being nasalisable. Similarly, G. *zu stehen* (to
stand) becomes 'tsu schteeə' and 'tsu schtee,;' G. *zu thun*
(to do) may be 'tsu tuu,'—'tsu tuuə,' or (with *n* preserved)
'tsu tuunə,' and G. *gehen* (to go) may have the same phases.

§ 5. *The Consonants.*

The Germanism of confusing b, p; t, d; k, g, is present in
PG. and they are pronounced *flat*, that is, with more of the
surface of the organs in contact than in English—a characteristic which distinguishes German from languages of the Dutch
and Low-Saxon (Plattdeutsch) type.[1] This must be remem-
bered in reading the examples, in which the ordinary usage
of these letters will be nearly followed.

The consonants are b, ch, d, f, g (in *get*, *give*), gh, h, j
(English *y*), k, l, m, n, ng, p, r (trilled), s (in *seal*, not as in
miser), sch (in *ship*), t, w (a kind of *v* made with the lips alone).
'ch' has the two usual variations as in *recht* and *buch*, and its
sonant equivalent 'gh' (written with 'g' in German) presents
the same two phases, as in G. *regen* and *bogen.* 'ng' before a

---

[1] The real physiological generation of these *flat* consonants is very difficult for
an Englishman to understand. Dr. C. L. Merkel, of Leipzig, a middle-German,
confesses that for a long time he did not understand the pure b, d, not having
heard them in his neighbourhood. He distinguishes (*Physiologie der Mensch-
lichen Sprache*, Leipzig, 1866, pp. 146-156), 1. The "soft shut sounds" or
mediæ, characterized by an attempt to utter voice before the closure is released,
2. "the half-hard shut sounds" or *tenues implosivæ*, characterized by a sound
produced by compressing the air in the mouth by the elevation of the larynx, the
glottis being closed, which " therefore acts like a piston," followed by the sudden
opening of the mouth and glottis, allowing the vowel to pass, (this is his description of the *flat* sounds, which he says Brücke, a Low-Saxon, reckons among his
mediæ), 3. "the hard explosive shut sounds," characterized by a shut mouth
and open glottis through which the unvocalised breath is forced against the
closing barrier more strongly than in the last case, but without pressure from the
diaphragm ; 4. "the aspirated or sharpened explosive sound," in which the last
pressure occurs with a jerk. The compound English distinction, p, b; t, d; k, g,
seem almost impossible for a middle and south-German to understand.—A. J. E.

vowel as in *singer*, hence ' finger ' is *fing-er* and not *fing-ger*.
' n ' before ' k ' is like ' ng,' as in G. *links* (on the left), which
is pronounced like an English syllable. Vowels to be repeated
are indicated by a hyphen, as in ge-ennərt (altered), nei-ichkeit (novelty).

Should letters be wanted for English j, z, v, w, the first
may have *dzh*, and the others italic *z*, *v*, *w*, with ks for x.

As the reader of English who speaks PG. can learn the
German alphabetic powers in half an hour, PG. should be
written on a German basis, and not according to the vagaries
of English spelling, with its uncertainty and reckless sacrifice
of analogy. In print, PG. should appear in the ordinary
roman type, in which so many German books are now published.[1]

§ 6. *Stein or Schtein?*

The sequents *sp*, *st*, are perhaps universally converted into
' schp ' and ' scht ' in PG., as in ' geescht ' for *gehest*, ' hascht '
for *hast*, ' Kaschp'r' for *Caspar*, ' schtee͏' for *stein*, and 'schpeck'
for *speck*, all of which are genuine German, as distinguished
from Saxon, Anglosaxon, and Hollandish, because *S is incompatible before labials* (w, m, p) *and dentals* (l, n, t) *in High
German*. Hence, where Dutch has *zwijn*, *smidt*, and *spcelen*,
German has *schwein*, *schmidt*, and *schpielen;* and for Dutch
forms like *slijm*, *snee*, and *steen*, German has *schleim*, *schnee*,
and *schtein;* but as the German uses the conventional spell-
ings ' spielen ' and ' stein,' he is apt to fancy that a law of
speech is of less importance than the flourishes of a writing-
master, or the practice of a printing-office, even when his own
speech should teach him the law.

That German has this feature practically, is proved by the
fact that words apparently in sp-, st-, become schp-, scht-,
when adopted into Russian, although this language has initial
sp-, st-,—a transfer of *speech* rather than of *spelling*, which is
as old as the thirteenth century, when the Old High German

---

[1] On the inconsistencies of Rauch's Orthography on an English basis, see my
note 2, p. 655 of Ellis's *Early English Pronunciation*.

'spiliman' (an actor) went into Old Slavonic as (using German spelling) 'schpiljman,' where 'spiljman' would have been more in accordance with the genius of the language.

§ 7. *Vowel Changes.*

Altho the pronunciation of many words is strictly as in High German, there are the following important variations. German *a* becomes normally the vowel of *what* and *fall*, but it has the Swiss characteristic of closing to ' o,' as in ' ool' (eel) G. *aal*; ' ee, mool' (once) G. *ein mal*; ' woor' (true) G. *wahr;* 'joor' (year) G. *jahr;* ' froogha' (to ask) G. *fragen;* ' frook' (a question) G. *frage;* ' doo' (there) G. *da;* 'schloofa' (to sleep) G. *schlafen;* ' schtroos' (street) G. *strasze;* ' nooch' (towards) G. *nach;* ' hoor' (hair) G. *haar*, but ' paar' (pair) and others do not change.

The vowel of *fat* occurs in ' kschær' (harness) G. *geschirr;* ' hærpscht' (autumn) G. *herbst;* færtl (fourth) G. *viertel;* kærl (fellow) G. *kerl.*

German ' o' becomes ' u,' as in ' kuma' (*u* short, see § 2) *to come*, Austrian kuma, G. *kommen;* ' schun' (already) G. *schon;* ' fun' (of) G. *von;* ' wuuna' (to reside) G. *wohnen;* ' wuu' (where) G. *wo;* ' sun' (sun) Austr. sunn, G. *sonne;* ' suu,' and ' suun' (son) G. *sohn;* ' númitaag' and ' nómidaak' (afternoon) G. *nachmittag;* 'dunarschtaag' (thursday) G. *donnerstag;* ' hunich' (honey) G. *honig.*

German ' ei' is often ' ee,' as in ' heem' (home) G. *heim;* ' deel' (part) G. *theil;* ' seef' (soap) G. *seife;* ' bleech' (pale) G. *bleich;* eens (one) G. *eins;* ' tswee' (two) G. *zwei.*

Irregular forms appear in ' maulwarf' (mole) G. *maulwurf;* ' blĕs' (pale, rhyming *lace*) G. *blass;* ' siffer' (tippler) G. *säufer;* ' schpoot' (late) G. *spät*, ä long ; ' m'r wella' (we will) G. *wir wollen;* ' dii úmeesa' (the ant) G. *die ameise;* ' ep,' ' eb ' (whether) G. *ob;* ' dærfa' (to dare) G. *dürfen;* ' færichtarlich ' (frightful) G. *fürchterlich;* ' ich færicht mich dat [or dart, G. *dort*] ana tsu gee,.' *I fear me to go yonder.*

' Dat ana' is for G. *dort hin*, ' ana' being a Swiss adverb made of G. *an* (on, towards). 'dat' is not common in PG. and it may have been brought from abroad, as it occurs in Suabian—

"Aepfel hott ma dott gsia, wie d' Kirbiss bey üss;" (Radlof, 2, 10.)—(Man hat dort gesehen) *Apples have been seen there like* (G. Kürbisse, PG. kærəpsə) *pumpkins with us.*

The foregoing 'anə' appears in Swiss "ume und anne" (thither and hither) where 'ume,' Austr. 'uma,' is from G. *um* (about). Stalder refers 'anne' to G. *an-hin,* and Swiss 'abe' to *ab-hin.* Schmid (Schwäb. Wb., p. 23) has ane, dortane, dettane. Schmeller (Bayer. Wb. 1869, p. 91) cites Graff (1, 499), for Ohg. *ostana* (from the East), and Grimm (3, 205).

While PG. 'alt' and 'kalt' (old, cold, *a* in wh*a*t) have the comparatives 'eltər,' 'keltər,' the influence of *r* in 'karts' (short), G. *kurz,* and 'hart' (hard), produces 'kœrtsər' and 'hærtər,' instead of G. *kürzer* and *härter.* Long *a* becomes long *u* in G. *samen* (seed), PG. 'suumə.'

§ 8. *Dipthong Changes.*

German 'au' sometimes becomes 'aa' (in call), as in PG. 'laafə' (to walk) G. *laufen;* 'glaabə' (to believe) G. *glauben;* 'kaafə' (to buy) G. *kaufen;* 'tsaam' (bridle) G. *zaum;* 'traam' (dream) G. *traum;* 'fraa' (wife, woman) G. *frau,* PG. pl. 'weiwər,' because, as the German plural of *frauen* could not well make 'fraaə,' the plural of *weib* was preferred.

German 'au' remains in PG. 'plaum' (plum) G. *pflaume;* 'daum' (thumb); 'haufə' (heap); 'saufə' (to sup); 'haus' (house); 'taub' (dove) G. *taube;* 'aus' (out); 'fauscht' (fist).

German 'au' becomes 'oo' (Eng. floor) in PG. 'groo' (grey) an earlier form of G. *grau;* 'bloo' (blue) G. *blau;* and the name 'Stauffer' is sometimes pronounced 'stoof'r.'

In the plural, 'au' becomes 'ei,' as in PG. 'haus,' pl. 'heiser;' 'maus' pl. 'meis;' 'laus' pl. 'leis;' 'maul' (mouth) pl. 'meiler' G. pl. *mäuler;* 'gaul,' pl. 'geil,' G. pl. *gäule* (horses); 'sau' (sow, hog), pl. 'sei,' G. pl. *säue, sauen.*

When 'au' has become 'aa' the German plural *äu* becomes 'ee,' as in 'beem' (trees) G. *bäume;* 'tseem' (bridles) G. *zäume.*

' Floo,' G. *floh* (flea) pl. ' flee' for G. *flöhe*, is due to the fact that German long ö is replaced by ee.

German *au* is *u* in the earlier PG. ' uf ' (up) G. *auf*, found in Swisserland and other localities ; but ' haus ' is not *hūs*, and ' maul ' is not *mūl* as in Swiss.

§ 9.   *Words lengthened.*

Some monosyllables are dissyllabised under the influence of trilled *r*, and of *l* (which is akin to *r*), as in ' Jar'ik ' (York) ; ' Jær'ik,' German *Georg* (George), perhaps the only example of the Berlin change of G to (German) J.

PG.	G.	E.	PG.	G.	E.
schtar'ik	stark	*strong*	dar'ich	durch	*through*
mar'ikt	markt	*market*	kar'əp	korb	*basket*
ær'əwət	arbeit	*work*	bær'ik	berg	*hill*
kær'ich	kirche	*church*	mil'ich	milch	*milk*
karrich	karren	*cart*	kal'ich	kalk	*lime*
geenə	gehen	*to go*	genunk	genug	*enough*
reeghərə	regnen	*to rain*	wamməs	wamms	*jacket*

PG. g'seenə (seen) G. *gesehen*, occurs in South German, as in the following (Radlof 2, 100), which closely resembles PG.

. . . . vun der Zit an het me niks me vun em g'sehne un g'hört. *From that time on,* (' mĕ' G. man) *one* (hat) *has seen and heard nothing* (' mē' G. mehr) *more of him.*

G. Es fängt an zu regnen und zu schneien.   PG. es fangt (not fängt) aa, tsu recghərə un tsu schneeə.   *It begins to rain and to snow.*

§ 10.   *Words shortened.*

Condensation is effected by absorption, as of *d* by *n* in ' wunər' (wonder) G. *wunder ;* and of *f* by *p* in ' kəp' (head) G. *kopf ;*—by the elision of consonants (an Austrian feature) as in ' wet ' (would) G. *wollte ;* ' net' (not) G. *nicht.*

By elision of vowels (particularly final *e*) as in ' schuul' (school) G. *schule,* ' tsammə' (together) G. *zusammen ;* and by shortening vowels, as in ' siw'o ' (seven) G. *sieben ;* ' gew'o ' (to give) G. *gēben ;* G. *heurathen* (to marry), Suab. heuren, PG. ' heiərə '; G. *gleich* (like) PG. ' glei'; ' tsimlich ' (tolerable) G. *ziemlich.*

PG.	G.	E.	PG.	G.	E.
niks	nichts	*nothing*	mr sin	wir sind	*we are*
wet	wollte	*would*	géscht'r	gestern	*yesterday*
set	sollte	*should*	nemmə	nehmen	*to take*
knəp	knopf	*button*	nam'itag	nachmittag	*afternoon*
knep	knöpfe	*buttons*	geblíwə	geblieben	*remained*
kich	küche	*kitchen*	jets ¹	jetzt	*now*
kuuchə	küchen	*cake*	parr'ə	pfarrer	*preacher*
wəch	woche	*week*	oowət	abend	*evening*
wəchə	wochen	*weeks*	weipsleit	weibsleute	*women*
kiw'l	kübel	*bucket*	rei,	herein	*herein*
blos	blase	*bladder*	nei,	hinein	*hither-in*
meim	meinem	*to my*	draa,	daran	*thereon*
anər	ander	*other*	eltscht	älteste	*oldest*
nanər	einander	*each other*	tswíwlə	zwiebeln	*onions*
unər	unter	*under*	hend	hände	*hands*
drunə	darunter	*ther' under*	plets	plätze	*places*
nunər	hinunter	*down there*	nummə ¹	nun mehr	*only*
dro'wə	daroben	*above*	nimmə ¹	nimmer	*never*
driw'ə	darüber	*ther' over*	mee ¹	mehr	*more*
drin	darin	*ther' in*	noo	darnach	*ther' after*
ruff	darauf	*there up*	pluuk	pflūg	*plow*
nuff	hinauf	*up there*	plíighə	pflüge	*plows*
sind	sünde	*sin*	kalénər	kalénder	*cdlendar*

As G. 'ü' becomes 'i' in PG., G. *lügen* (to tell a lie) and *liegen* (to lie down—both having the first vowel long) might be confused, but the latter is shortened in PG., as in 'ær likt' (he lies down) 'ær liikt' (he tells a lie).

PG. Was wi' t? *What wilst thou?* G. Was willst du?
Woo't weepe? Woo't fight? Woo't teare thy selfe? ²
Ich wil fischə gee,. *I will go to fish.*
Ich hab kschriwwə. *I have (geschrieben) written.*
Sin mr net keiərt? *Are we not married?* G. Sind wir nicht geheirathet?
(or verheirathet.)

Infinitive -n is rejected, as in the Swiss and Suabian dialects. In an Austrian dialect it is rejected when *m, n,* or *ng* precedes, as in singa, rena, nehma, for *singen, rennen, nehmen.—Castelli*, Wörterbuch, 1847, p. 31.

The length of some vowels is doubtful, as in 'rot' or 'root' (red, like English *rŏte* or *rōde*), 'so' or 'soo,' 'nochbər' or 'noochbər,' 'əmol' or 'əmool,' 'ja' or 'jaa,' 'sii' or 'sĭ' (she, they, ĭ in deceĭt, not in *sit*). Compare English 'Sēe!' and 'Sĕe thêre !'

Accent in PG. agrees with that of High German. When indicated, as in danóot or danoot' (for the 'oo' represent a single vowel, as in Eng. *floor*), it is to afford aid to the reader not familiar with German accent.

¹ Swiss forms.
² *Hamlet*, act 5, sc. 1, speech 106 ; folio 1623, tragedies, p. 278, col. 2.

CHAPTER III.

VOCABULARY.

The vocabulary of PG. has but few synonyms, a single word being used where High German has several, as 'plats' (place) for G. *platz* and *ort.* Of the German words for *horse* (pferd, ross, gaul, etc.), 'gaul' is universal in speech, *ross* seems not to be known, and *pferd* is almost restricted to print.[1] A colt is not called *füllen* as in German, but 'hutsch,' with a diminutival 'hutschli' (in Suabian *hutschel, hutschele,* Westerwald *husz,* Lusatian *huszche.*)

A pig is not *ferkel* (Lat. porc-ell-us, Welsh porch-ell) but 'seili' (from *sau*), and children call it 'wuts' (Suab. butzel) a repetition of this being used (as well in vicinal English) in calling these animals. 'Kalb' (calf, pl. 'kelwər') is named by children 'haməli'[2] when a suckling. Cows are called with 'kum see! see! see haməli! see!' and when close at hand with 'suk suk suk' (as in for*sook*)—used also in the English of the locality.[3] Of G. *knabe* (boy) and *bube,* pl. *buben,* PG. takes the latter as 'buu,' pl. 'buuwə;' and of the G. *haupt* and *kopf* (head) it prefers the latter as 'kəp.' Of the verbs *schmeissen* and *werfen* (to throw), *kriegen* and *bekommen* (to obtain), *hocken* and *sitzen* (to sit), *schwetzen* and *sprechen* (to talk), *erzählen* and *sagen* (to tell), PG. uses 'schmeissə,' 'kriighə,' 'həkə,' 'schwetsə' and 'saaghə' almost exclusively.

The suffix -lein, condensed to -li and -l, is the universal diminutival, as in Swisserland and South Germany—a small

---

[1] Of words not occurring in print, the Swiss, Bavarian, and Suabian form bruntsen replaces harnen and its synonyms.
[2] Seemingly akin to Swiss *ammeli, mammeli* (a child's sucking-glass), whence *mämmelen* (to like to drink). G. amme (a wet-nurse), in Bavaria, also a mother.
[3] PG. des kalb sukt (this calf sucks,) G. *saugt.*

house being called 'heissli' and not *häus-chen*, and a girl 'meedl' and not *mädchen*. It is, however, very often associated with the adjective klee, (little) G. *klein*, as in PG. 'ə klee, bichli ' (a little book).

German *kartofeln* (potatoes) is rejected for G. *grundbirncn*[1] under the form of 'krumpiirə,' where 'krum' is accepted by some as *krumm* (crooked), while some regard the latter part as meaning *pears*, and others as *berries*.

F'rleícht, Fileícht (perhaps, G. vielleicht) are in use, but the former seems the more common.

Sauərampl, G. sauerampfer (sorrel, Rumex).

Rewwər, Krik, Krikli (Eng. *river, creek*) have thrust aside G. *flusz* and *bach*.

Laafə (to walk ; G. *laufen* to run, and to walk).

Schpring-ə (to run, a Swiss usage. G. *springen*, to leap, spring, gush).

Petsə (to pinch), Alsace pfetsə, Swiss pfätzen, Suab. pfetzen.

Tref (Suab., a knock, blow). PG. 'ich tref dich' (I strike thee).

Schmuts (a hearty kiss). Swiss, Suab., in G. *schmatz*.

Un'ich (under), G. unter, occurs in provincial German as unn-ig and unt-ig ; hinnig occurs also, PG. 'hinnich,' as in 'hinnich d'r diir' *behind the door*.

> Wii m'r donaus gləffə sin, bin ich hinnich iin nooch gləffə. *As we walked out, I walked behind him.*

For 'hinnich,' Alsatian has hing-ə, as in 'M'r geen hing-ə [nach den] noo də goortə noo'— *We go along behind the garden*.

Uumət, oomət, Austr. omad, Swiss amet, G. das grummet (aftermath). Suab. ämt, emt, ömd, aumad ; Bavar. âmad.

Arik, arrig (much, very), Swiss arig, G. arg (bad, cunning).

> PG. Ich hab net gwist [Suab. gwest] dass es so arrik reeghərt. *I did not suppose it to be raining so hard.*

Artlich (tolerably) is the Swiss *artlich* and *artig*.

Ewwə, G. adv. ēben (really, even, just), but it is PG. 'eewə' when it is the adj. *even*.

> Ich hab ewwə net gwist for sure eb ær ə fraa hət ədər net. (*Rauch.*) *I did not even know 'for sure' if he has a wife or not.*

ámanat, adv. metathesised and adapted from G. *an einem Orte* (at a place), a dative for an accusative *an einen Ort* (in a place) as

---

[1] This name seems to have been originally applied to the crooked tubers of the Jerusalem artichoke, and *humming-bird* was probably applied to moths of the genus *Sphinx* (named from the form of the larva) before the bird bearing this name was known in Europe.

used here. In the example, 'ana' is G. *an* inflected, and *să* of *zu schicken* is omitted, as sometimes done in PG.

... wan als a briif kummt f'r âmanat ana schike ... (*Rauch*.) *When ever a letter comes for to send on*—to be sent on.

Henkweida (weeping willow). G. Hängebirke, is hanging birch.

Tappar (quickly), as in Schpring tappar *run quick! be in a hurry*—thus used in Westerwald, and as *very* in Silesia. G. tapfer (brave, bravely), E. dapper.

Meenar (more), **Meenscht** (most), for G. *mehr, meist*, are réferable to *mancher* and a hypothetic *mannigste*. 'Mee' and 'mee,' (more), Swiss—"Was wett i meh?" *What would I more.* "Nimme meh," *never more.* PG. 'Was wet ich mee? Nimmi mee.' (See *Ellis*, Early English Pronunciation, p. 663, note 39.)

Schtrublich, schtruwlich. G. *struppig* (bristly, rough), Swiss *strublig*, PG. 'schtruwlich' (disordered, uncombed, as hair). English of the locality *stroobly*.

Neewich; SG. *nebensich*, Wetterau (upper Hessia) *nébig*, G. *neben* (beside).

"Naevvich der mommy ruht er now [Eng. *now*]
In sellem Gottes-acker [1] dort,
Shraegs [2] fun der Kreutz Creek Kerrich nuf, [hinauf.]
Uft denk ich doch an seller ort!"—*Rachel Bahn.*

Hensching, G. *handschue* (gloves, Sw. händschen) becomes a new word with 'hen' for *hände* (hands), the ü umlaut being used to pluralise, but the word is singular also, and, to particularise, a glove proper is 'fing-er hensching' and a mitten 'fauscht-hensching.' This termination is given to 'pœrsching' a peach.

Sidder (since), Swiss *sider, sitter*; Suabian and Silesian *sider*; Scotch, etc., *sithens.*

Schpel (a pin), SG. *die spelle* (a better word than G. stecknadel); Dutch *speld* (with *d* educed from *l*); Lat. SPIcuLa.

Botsar (masc. a tail-less hen), Holstein, *buttars*. Provincial G. *butzig* (stumpy).

Mallikap (i.e. thick-headed, a tadpole). Swiss *mollig, molli* (stout, blunt); Suabian *mollig* (fleshy). Alsatian muurkrentl (tadpole) from muur, G. moder, Eng. *mud.* The PG. of western New York has taken the New England word *polliwog.*

Blech (tin, a tin cup); dim. 'blechli.' Blechiche Bool (a tin *bowl*, i.e. a *dipper*, a convenient word which seems not to have been introduced). In Pennsylvanian English, a tin cup is *a tin.*

[1] Scarcely legitimate, the PG. word for a grave-yard being kærich-hof.
[2] Diagonally.

In old English, 'than' represented *than* and *then*, and PG. has
' dann ' for both G. *dann* (then) and *denn* (for); and also ' wann ' for
wann (when) and *wenn* (if), as in Rachel Bahn's lines—

"Doch guckt 's ah recht huebsch un' Doch gukt 's aa recht hipsch un
nice ' neis'
Wann all die Baehm sin so foll ice—" Wan al dii beem sin so fol eis—
Yet it looks (auch) *also right fair and ' nice'* when *all the trees are so full of ice.*

" Forn bild der reinheit is 's doh, F'r 'n bild dar reinheit [1] iss es doo,
In fact, mer kenne sehne noh, ' in fækt,' m'r kenne seene noo,
Dass unser Hertz' [2] so rein muss seik, dass unser hærts so rein [1] muss sei,,
Wann in des Reich mer welle neih." wann in des reich m'r welle nei,.

For a picture of purity is it (da) *here, ' in fact'* (wir können sehen darnach) *we
can perceive therefrom, that our heart must be as pure,* (wenn in das reich wir
wollen hinein) if *we would enter into the kingdom.*

Baschte (to husk maize), from ' bascht,' G. *bast* (soft inner bark,
E. bast), applied in PG. to the husk of Indian corn.—Rachel
Bahn (1869) thus uses it—

"Die leut sie hocke's welshcorn ab, Dii leit sii hacke 's welschkarn ap,
'S is 'n rechte guhte crop, 's iss 'n rechte guute ' crap,' (fem.)
Un' wann's daer genunk werd sei, un wan 's dærr genunk wært sei,,
Noh bashte sies un' fahres eih." noo baschte sii 's un faare 's ei,.

The people they (ab-hacken) *chop off* ('s, das) *the maize,* (es ist) *it is a right
good ' crop,' and when* (es) *it becomes* (dürr genug) *dry enough, they* (darnach)
afterwards husk it and (fahren) *haul it in.*

Greisslich (to be disagreeably affected). SG. grüselig, G. gräszlich
(horrible), E. grisly.

Noo, danoo', danoot', nord, G. darnach (then, subsequently).

Bendl (a string), schuubendl (shoe-string). Swiss bändel.

Schteiper, n. (Lat. stîpes), a prop, as of timber. G. nautical term
steiper, a stanchion. **Schteipere,** v.t. to prop; to set a prop.

Ferhúttele, v. intrans. ' Ich bin f'r-huttlt,' (I am confused, per-
plexed.) ' Ich denk dii bissnoss iss 'n bissli f'r-huttlt.' (I think
the ' business' is a bit mixed up.) G. verhüdeln (to spoil, bungle.)

Paanhaas, as if, G. *pfanne-hase* (pan-hare). Maize flour boiled in
the metsel-soup, afterwards fried and seasoned like a *hare.* (Compare Welsh *rabbit.*) The word is used in English, conjointly
with *scrapple.*

Loos (a sow), as in Swiss and Suabian.

Laad, fem. (coffin), toodlaad, toodolaad, as in Alsace. G. die lade
(chest, box, case). PG. bettlaad, Suab. bettlade, for G. bettge-
stell (bedstead).

---

[1] By analogy these words should be rei, and rei,heit, but as they are scarcely
PG. they are given as High German.
[2] This word is correct without the elisive mark, which perverts the syntax.

Schtreel, m. (a comb), Swiss, Alsatian, Suab. der strähl. But G. striegel, PG. striegel, PG. strigl, is a currycomb.

Aarsch, the butt end of an egg, as in Suabian.

Falsch (angry), as in Swiss, Bavarian, and Austrian. PG. Sel hat mich falsch g'macht. *That made me angry.*

Hoochtsich, Alsat. hoochtsitt, G. hochzeit (a wedding).

Heemeln, Swiss heimeln (to cause a longing, to cause home feelings).

" Wie hämelt mich do alles a' !	Wii heemlt mich doo alles aa, !
Ich steh, un denk, un guck;	ich schtee, un denk, un gukk;
Un was ich schier vergessa hab,	un was ich schiir f'rgessa hab,
Kummt wider z'rück, wie aus seim Grab,	kummt widd'r tsrik, wii aus seim graab,
Un steht do wie e' Spook !" *Harb.*	un schteet doo wii e schpukk !

(G. Wie alles da anheimelt mich) *How all here impresses me with home, I stand, and think, and look ; and what I had almost forgotten, comes back again as out of its grave, and stands here like a ghost.*

Drəp, pl. **drep** (simpleton, poor soul). "O du armer Tropff!" (Suabian). *Radlof,* 2, 10. "Die arma Drep!"—*Harbaugh.*

Schwalme (Swiss, for G. schwalbe, a swallow).

Jaa (O. Eng. yes), is used in answer to affirmative questions.

Joo (O. Eng. yea), is used in answer to negative questions. See Ch. viii. § 1, ¶ 12, and § 3, ¶ 2.

" Sin dü sachə dei, ? *Jaa,* sii sin." (Are the things thine ? *Yes,* they are.) "Sin dü sachə *net* dei, ? *Joo,* sii sin." (Are the things *not* thine. *Yea,* they are.) " Bischt du *net* g'sund ? *Joo,* ich bin."[1] (Are you *not* well ? *Yea, I am well.*)

saagt, G. *sagt* (he says): **secht,** as if G. sägt, for sagte (he said), as if it were a strong verb.

Gleich, to like, be fond of, Eng. to *like,* but perhaps not Eng. See Ch. viii., ¶ 3. PG. ær gleicht s geld—*he loves money.*

Glei, adv. (soon).—ær kummt glei—*he comes* (will be here) *directly.* Swiss *gly* and *gleich* have the same meaning.

Abartich, bartich, Ch. viii., § 3, ¶ 6 (adj. unusual, strange); (adv. especially). G. *abartig* degenerate.

" Der duckter sogt eara complaint wær . . . conclommereashen im kup, so dos se so unfergleichlich schwitza mus in der nacht, abbordich wan se tsu gedeckt is mit em fedder bet."—*Rauch,* Feb. 1, 1870. *The doctor asserts her 'complaint' to be . . . 'conglomeration' in the head, so that she must sweat uncommonly in the night,* PARTICULARLY *when she is covered [tsu is accented] in with the feather bed.*

Biibi, piipi, büibəli ; Swiss bibi, bibeli, bidli (a young chicken). Used also to call fowls—the second form in the vicinal English, in which a male fowl is often called a hé-biddy.

---

[1] The Rev. D. Ziegler.

The Swiss use in PG. of the genitive form *des* of the article, instead of the neuter nominative *das*, causes little or no confusion, because this genitive is not required, and its new use prevents confusion between *das* and *dasz*. Where German uses *des*, as in *Der Gaul des* (or *meines*) *Nachbars* (the horse of the, or my, neighbor), PG. uses a dative form—

... dem (or meim for meinem) nochbər sei, gaul (the neighbor his horse). See the quotation (p. 28) from Schöpf.

PG. inflects most of its verbs regularly, as in 'gedenkt' for G. *gedacht*, from *denken* (to think). In the following list, the German infinitive, as *backen* (to bake), is followed by the third person of the present indicative (er) *bäckt*, PG. (ær) 'bakt' (he bakes). The PG. infinitive of *blasen*, *braten*, *fragen*, *rathen*, *dürfen*, *verderben*, is 'bloosə, brootə, frooghə, rootə, dærfə, f'rdærwə.' 'bloosə˥ (to blow) and 'nemmə' (to take) occur below, in the extract from Miss Bahn.

G.	G.	PG.	G.	G.	PG.
blasen *blow*,	bläst	bloost	lesen *read*,	liest	leest
braten *bake*,	brät	broot	lassen *let*,	läszt	lesst
brechen, *break*,	bricht	brecht	messen *measure*,	miszt	messt
dreschen *thrash*,	drischt	drescht	nehmen *take*,	nimmt	nemmt
dürfen *dare*,	darf	dærf	rathen *advise*,	räth	root
fahren *drive*,	fährt	faart	saufen *tipple*,	säuft	sauft
fallen *fall*,	fällt	fallt	schelten *scold*,	schilt	schelt
fragen *ask*,	frägt	frookt	schlafen *sleep*,	schläft	schlooft
essen *eat*,	iszt	esst	schwellen *swell*,	schwillt	schwellt
fressen *devour*,	friszt	fresst	sehen *see*,	sieht	seet
geben *give*,	giebt	gept	stehlen *steal*,	stiehlt	schteelt
graben *dig*,	gräbt	graapt	tragen *carry*,	trägt	traagt
helfen *help*,	hilft	helft	verderben *spoil*,	verdirbt	f'rdærpt
laufen *run*,	läuft	laaft	vergessen *forget*,	vergiszt	f'rgesst

"Der wind, horch yuəht, wie er drum   D'r wint, harich juscht wii ær drum
bloss'd, ...   bloost, ...
Gar nix for ihm fersichert is,   Gaar niks f'r iim f'rsichərt iss,
Er nemmt sei aegner waek   ær nemmt sei, eegnər week,
Dorch ennich rissly geht er neih,   darich ennich rissli geet ær nei,
Un geht ah nuf die staek."   un geet aa 'nuf dii schteek.

The wind, just listen how it therefore (an expletive) *blows, ... quite nothing is secure for* (on account of) *him, he takes his* (eigener weg) *own way; through* (einig, einiges) *any crack he goes* (hinein) *in, and goes also* (hinauf) *up the* (stiege) *stair.*

The reader of PG. may be puzzled with 'ma' as used in "ous so ma subject ... mit ma neia Rail Road" (*Rauch*); 'fun mə' or 'fun əmə,' Ger. dative *von einem*, Old High German 'vone einemo;' G. *dem*, Ohg. 'demo;' G. *meinem*, Gothic

'meinamma,' which accounts for the final PG. vowel.　Miss
Bahn writes it ' mah '—

''S is noch so 'n anre glacner drup,	's iss noch so n anre gloenər drəp,
Mit so mah grosse dicke kup,	mit soo mə grossə dikkə kəp,
Der doh uf English screech-owl haest,	dær doo uf eng-lisch ' skriitsch-aul ' heest,
Der midde drin hut ah sei nesht.'	dær middə drin hot aa sei nescht.

*There is yet such another little fellow, with such a large thick head, this here
in English is called ' screech-owl,' the middle therein* [of the tree] *has also its nest.*

Remarking on "grosse dicke kup" in the second line, my
reverend friend Ziegler sends me the following declensions of
the united article and adjective.　The dative is used for the
genitive, as will appear in the chapter on Syntax.

Nom., Accus.	ən ('n) grosser dicker kopp,
Dat., Gen.	əmə ('mə) grossə dickə kopp.

Singular.

Nom.	der root wei,	.... iss guut.	*The red wine is good.*
Gen.	dem rootə wei,	... sei, farb is schee,.	
Dat.	„ „ „	.... hab ich 's tsu fərdankə.	
Acc.	dii rootə wei,	.... hat ær gedrunkə.	

Plural.

Nom.	dii rootə wei,	.... sin guut.	*The red wines are good.*
Gen.	dennə rootə woi,	... iir farb etc. (G. der rothen Weine Farbe ist schön.)	
Dat.	„ „ „	... hab ich 's etc. (G. den rothen Weinen.)	
Acc.	dii rootə wei,	.... hat ær, etc.	

CHAPTER IV.

GENDER.

§ 1. *Gender of English Words in Pennsylvania German.*

German gender and declension might be said to be in a
state of barbarism, were it not that some of the languages of
savages have refinements which are wanting in the tongues of
civilised people. German gender being in a high degree arbi-
trary and irrational, there seem but few principles applicable
to introduced words, and yet, the linguistic instinct produces
a measure of uniformity. The clear distinction in modern
English between a spring and a well, does not exist between
the German *der quell* (and *die quelle*, PG. 'dii qkel') and *der
brunnen*, but German has *der spring* also, which may be used
alone, or compounded in *springquell* or *springquelle*. Influenced by English, PG. uses 'dii schpring' for a natural spring
of water, keeping 'd'r brunnə' for a well, 'tsig-brunnə' for a
draw-well with a windlas and bucket—but also 'laafəndə
brunnə' for a spring.

As a German says 'dii' for the English article *the*, which
he hears applied to everything singular and plural, and as this
die is his own feminine and plural article, he will be likely to
say 'dii fens' for *the fence*, 'dii set' (set, of tools, etc.), 'dii
faundri' (foundry), 'dii bænk' (bank of a stream), 'dii færm'
(farm), 'dii plantaaschə' (plantation), 'dii téməti' (timothy
hay), 'dii portsch,' 'dii schtæmp ('stämp' in print, for G. *der
stempel*), 'dii watsch' (timepiece), 'dii *bel* hat geringt' (the
'bell' has 'rung'), "Stohrstube . . . mit einer offenen Front,"
(Store-room with an open front), "die *Fronte*[1] des Hauses"
(the 'front' of the house), "Die Sanitäts *Board*," "Eine *Lot*
Stroh," "Eine *Lotte* Grund," etc. All of these are feminine

---

[1] Such italics for English words are no part of the original.

in PG., together with the English nouns *alley, road, borough, square* (of a town) *fair, forge, creek* (a stream), *climate, bowl, vendue, court* (at law), *law, lawsuit, jury, yard* (of a house),—

Als Herr Yost . . . einen groszen Neufundländer Hund in seiner Y a r d [1] anders anbinden wollte, fiel ihn das Thier an . . . der Hund wieder an ihn sprang, und ihn gegen die F e n z [1] drängte, . . . *Der Pennsylvanier*, Lebanon, Pa. Sept. 1, 1869.

Of the masculine gender are *river* (PG. 'rewər'), *bargain, crop, beef* (but 'gedörtes beef' makes it neuter), *carpet, turnpike* (or *pike*), *store, gravel, shop, smith-shop, shed,* and of course words like *squire, lawyer,* and "*assignie.*"

Of the neuter gender are "*das främ*" (frame), " das *flaur* " (flour, influenced by G. *das mehl*), das *screen,* das *photograph,* das *piano,* das *supper,* das *buggy.*

Wishing to know the gender of the preceding English words in another county, the list was sent to the Rev. Daniel Ziegler, of York, Pa., who assigns the same genders to them, adding der *settee,* die *umbréll,* die *parasol,* die *bréssont* (prison), das *lampblack,* das *picter* (picture), das *candy,* das *cash,* das *lumber* (building timber), das *scantling,* das *parement,* das *township.*[2]

German *die butter* (butter) is masculine in PG. as in South Germany and Austria; and *die forelle* (the trout) is PG. 'dœr forél.' G. *die tunke* (gravy) is neuter under the form 'tunkəs' in PG., which makes the *yard* measure feminine, although in Germany (and in print here), it has been adopted as masculine.

Variations in grammatic gender are to be expected under the degenderising influence of English, but at present the

---

[1] This mode of indicating words is used to avoid corrupting the text with italics.

[2] As this essay is passing through the press, I add the following examples, which are all in print.

Der charter, deed (legal), humbug, lunch or lunsch, ein delikater Saurkraut-Lunch. Revenuctarif, crowd, fight, molasses, Select-Council, crop (fem. with Miss Bahn). Im Juli—schreit der Whipper-will.

Die jail, legislatur, Grandjury or grand Jury, ward (of a city), lane, toll, gate, pike or peik, bill (legislative), Cornetband or Cornet Band, eine grosze Box (of medicine), gefängniszbox, platform, manufactory, shelfing, counter.

Das County, committee or comite, picnic, screen (coal-screen), law (also fem.), trial, verdikt, basin (reservoir), Groszes Raffle für Turkeys und Gänse, ... ausgeraffelt werden.

German genders usually remain, as in *der stuhl* (chair), *der pflug* (plough, PG. 'pluuk'), *der trichter* (funnel, PG. 'trechter'), *der kork* (cork, PG. karik), *der indigo, der schwamm* (spunge), *die egge* (harrow, PG. ' eek,' sometimes ' êk'), *die bank* (bench), *die wiese* (meadow, PG. ' wiss'), *die kiste* (chest or chist, PG. kist), *das tüch* (cloth), *das messing* (brass, PG. ' měs,' like Eng. *mace*), *das füllsel* (stuffing, PG. ' filtsl').

§ 2. *The German Genders.*

In various aboriginal languages of America there are two genders, the animate and the inanimate—with a vital instead of a sexual polarity; and while German can and does associate gender and sex, its departure from this system is marked by objects conspicuously sexual, which may be of the neuter gender, and by sexless objects of the three genders.

It is easy to see why *das kind* (the child) is neuter, but under the ordinary view of the rise of grammatic gender, it is not easy to see why, in modern German, *der leib* (body) should be masculine, and *das weib* (woman, wife) of the same gender as the child—why *die liebe* (love) should be feminine, and *der friede* (peace) masculine. In German, the genders are incongruous, in English they are congruous, the masculine and feminine being correlatives, with correlative relations to the neuter also, and by dropping the false nomenclature of the German genders, we may be able to get a more philosophic view of them as they now exist, independently of the Old High German system of gender and declension, which accounts for their later condition.

If we adopt *strong* for the German masculine gender, there would be nothing gained if the feminine were called weak, but with the first as *strong*, the second as *soft*, and the third as *dull*, we would have three terms which do not suggest correlation or sex, and we might see nothing irrational in the fact that *man* might be of the strong, and *woman* of the dull gender; and that *peace* might be strong, and *love* soft.

Of the *strong* gender are mann, dieb, freund, mord, mund, hase (of energetic action), aal, salm, fisch, tisch (δίσκος), käse (CASEUS), schnee, klei, stock, fink (a strong-billed bird), apfel (naturally harsh), stahl, stiefel, schuh, strumpf, fusz, keil, bart, baum, daum, dorn,[1] punkt, stich, begfnn, rubin, diamant, klump, kummer, verstand, name, tag, halm (a rough material), floh, krebs, skorpion, hummer, hals, fels, saft, bau, rath, werth, zoll, flusz, Rhein, raub, acker, bogen.

Of the *soft* gender are birne, hand, historie (Lat. -IA), liebe, hoffnung, woh-nung, stadt, burg (implying also jurisdiction), sonne, gluth, milch, rahm, amsel, drossel, butter, feder, gans, maus, ratte, luft, frucht, nacht, macht (as if personi-fied), armuth, kraft, furcht, kunst, haut, frau, wurst, schnur, bahn, marsch, welt.

Of the *dull* gender are weib, grab, brod,[2] blei, eisen, gold, silber, zinn, (but der zink,) geld, feld, land, vieh, pferd (the type being agricultural), rind, joch, pech, haar, auge, bein, dorf, ding, mensch, mädchen, volk, hirn, leben, wort, buch, gesetz, herz, gemach, loth, glück, werk, beil, messer, schwert, glas, fenster, feuer, licht, wetter, wasser, bier, malz, kraut, lamm, ei, haupt, kalb, loch.

[1] From a Gothic masculine in -us,—*das horn* being from a Gothic neuter in -n.
[2] Primitive bread was probably rather heavy than light—if a mnemonic view may be taken.

CHAPTER V.

§ 1. The English Infusion.

Pennsylvania German has long been recognised as a dialect with certain English words, which are sometimes inflected in the German manner. Sportive examples were quoted in the last century, and one is occasionally cited as characteristic, which occurs in Joh. Dav. Schöpf's Travels (1783-4) published at Erlangen, in 1788, and thus quoted by Radlof,[1] but in German characters :—

"Mein Stallion ist über die Fehnsz getscheumpt, und hat dem Nachbor sein whiet abscheulich gedämatscht." (My *stallion jumped* over the *fence* and horribly *damaged* my neighbor's *wheat*.)

This example is probably spurious and a joke, because PG. 'hengscht' and 'weetsə' (instead of *stallion* and *wheat*) are in common use—for the Pennsylvania farmer uses German terms for introduced European objects, and if he calls *rye* 'karn' (G. korn), instead of *roggen*, this itself is a German name for what is in some localities regarded as corn by excellence. Another example of Schöpf has 'geklaret land' (cleared land), and 'barghen' (bargain), which are correct.

The German brings with him a vocabulary which is not quite adapted to the objects around him, and he improves his language by dropping such of his words as have an indefinite meaning, replacing them with terms which have an exact and scientific value, where High German is weak and indefinite— having failed to Latinise its vocabulary at the revival of learning. The Pennsylvanian uses 'fenss' or 'fents' (not "fehnsz") for the English *fence*, because the German *zaun* is equally a *hedge*; he uses 'flaur' (or 'flauer' Eng. flour) as well as the German *mehl*, because the latter is equivalent to English meal ; he seizes upon *bargain* as better than anything in his vernacu-

---

[1] Mustersaal aller teutschen Mund-arten, . . . Bonn, 1822, vol. 2, p. 361. By a type error, *m* of getscheumpt was omitted. See also Dr. Mombert's History of Lancaster County, Pennsylvania, 1869, p. 373.

lar; and he restricts G. *wagen* (with the sound of ' wagha') to *wagon*, adopting a variation like "bändwagen" for a vehicle used by a musical band, using ' kerritsch ' (" carriagemacher") for the English *carriage*, altho ' kutsch' (G. kutsche) is also in use. He adopts English expressions for clearing land and speaks of a *clearing* (which he makes feminine) because the destruction of forests by chopping and burning is not a European practice. Railroads were probably built in America before they were in use in Germany, and in Pennsylvania, our English name was imitated in ' reelroot ' (' Plankenroad ' is in print) or, as in many other cases, the word was translated into "riegelweg." At a later date the foreign name "eisenbahn" was brought in by later immigrants—and " riegel-bahn" is in use.

§ 2. *Newspapers.*

The Pennsylvania German appreciates humor, and to avoid the humorous and often illegitimate use of English words, the first examples in these pages will be selected from the advertisements of about a dozen different newspapers, all printed in the barbarous German character, and published at distant points in Pennsylvania. In such compositions, the attention of the public is called to common objects in a vocabulary which can be accepted without hesitation, and in a style somewhat above the colloquial, in which a horse is called ' gaul ' and not *pferd* (' pfœrt ') as usual in print. The spelling is sometimes English and sometimes more or less Germanised, without much affecting the pronunciation, as in " store" (a retail shop [1]) or "stohr" (buchstore, storehalter, stohrhaus), which are equally ' schtoor'; "frame," (främe, främ, frühm), are equally the English *frame;* " schap " (shap, schop, schopp, shop, pl. schöp) ; "township" (townschip, taunschip): "county" and "caunty"; "turnpike" and "turnpeik"; "cash " and " casch."

In some localities, English names of streets like *King, Queen, High, Water, Chesnut Street*, are used in German speech and print, and in others, *Königstrasze, Quienstrasze, Highstrasze, Wasserstrasze* and *Chesnutstrasze*, are preferred.

---

[1] See note 1 on next page.

As parenthetic words like (Dry Goods) occur in the originals, explanations will be [in brackets], and attention will be called to strictly English words by putting them in *italics*.

The " Pennsylvanische Staats-Zeitung " (published at Harrisburg, the State Capital) claims a larger circulation than any English journal of that city, and the number for Nov. 25, 1869, will be quoted here in the original spelling. Here, where English introduced words might be expected throughout, certain French words are adopted from the German dictionaries, such as *reparaturen, delikatessen,* lagerbier *salon* (also *saloon*)[1] *etablissement, engagiren, quotiren, instruiren, autorisiren, ordonnanz.* Others are rather English than French, as *pavements, arrangements, publikationspreisen, textbücher, jury, city, controle* (. . . so wie dasz die City alleinige Controle über denselben Committeé . . . .), *connektion, construktion, order, governör, provisionen, groceries.*

Beste Familien-Mehl, in Fässern [in another journal—Roggen*flauer per bärrel—preim flaur*] *superfine per Bärrel ; Prime* weitzen *;* Roggen [rye] *per Buschel.* Korn [maize or indian corn, properly called Welschkorn in the same column under the quoted Lancaster prices, where " Korn" means rye.] Hafer *; Middlings ; Shorts.*

In the Price-current we find—

Fische . . . *Rock* [Labrax lineatus]; *Pike* [for Hecht, pl. Hechte, a known term] ; *Halibut ; Haddock ; Sturgeon ; Trout ; White Perch* [Labrax albus, vel mucronatus] ; Weisze Fische [Coregonus albus] ; Härringe ; *Cat*fische [Pimelodus, more commonly called ' katsəfisch'].

Fleische . . . *Roast Beef per* Pfund ; *Rump Steaks ; Surloin ;* Hammelfleisch ; Schweinfleisch ; Gedörrtes *Beef* [Getrocknetes Rindsfleisch is quoted from Pittsburg]; *Beef* Schinken ; . . . *Mess Pork* ; . . . Schmalz in *kegs ; Lard*-Oel ; Butter (roll . . . print) [with 'roll' and ' 'print' in Roman type]; Molasses [commonly called məlássich] ; Süszkartoffeln [a translation of sweet-potatoes, instead of bataten] ; *Schellbarks* [nuts of the shell-bark hickory] ; Aepfelbutter (Latwerg) [G. Latwerge, PG. lâtwærik, translated from E. apple-butter].

In the humorous department we find—

Ein ähnliches Räthsel wie sell eine, war scho [schon] früher im *Päper* ; . . . Sie sind gemuvt ?[2] *Very well,* . . . Sell isch e guat's[3] Plätzel . . . sellem Joseph am Eck[4] lasse mer nix [lassen wir nichts] zu leids thun ; . . .

[1] Any place where liquor is retailed is called a saloon, and in a certain town a cabin with a single room is labeled DON JUAN WALLING'S SIGN EMPORIUM.
[2] ' You have *removed*' (your residence), but the third person plural is not thus used in PG.   [3] G. ein gutes, but the Austrian extension *gŭăt* is not PG.
[4] Neuter for feminine, as in Bavarian and Austrian.

The next examples are condensed from journals of various localities, all printed in the German character. The spelling and use of italics as before.

Der Grosze Wohlfeile *Dry Goods Store*. Jetzt eröffnet: Direkt von New York; *Bärgens* in Weiszgütern und Ellenwaaren (Dry Goods), Gemischte *Mohairs*; Schöne *Dress Ginghams*; *Long Cloth* [another has Langes Tuch].

Country Orders werden mit *prompt*heit ausgeführt . . . Groszhandels oder *Wholesäle* Preisen zu *Retail*en oder einzelnen [others have "im groszen und kleinen," "Groz und Klein-Verkauf"] . . . *Ingrain* oder Blumiger *Kärpet*; . . . *Entry* und Treppen [stair] *Carpets*; *Cottage-Carpets*; *Floor* Oel-Tücher [another has Boden-Oeltücher]; Marseilles und *Honeycomb Quilts*; *Matting*, weisz und bunt.

Allgemeine *Stohr*güter; Tücher für *Ladies Cloaks* [another has Damen *Cloak*stoffe.] . . . *Lädies Dress-Goods* [others have *Dress*güter, *Dress*-Anzüge, *Dress*waaren]; *Fäncy*-Waaren; Ueberdecken; *Quilts* und Tisch-*Diapers*; *Napkins*; *Ticking* beim Stück; *Carriage Trimmings*; Extra grosze *gequilte comfortables*; *Blänkets*; *Counter Paints* [counterpanes]; *Dry Goods* für Frühjahr und Sommer. Kein *Humbug*.

Millinery Waaren; *Ladies-*, *Misses-*, und Kinder Stroh und *Fäncy Bonnets* und *Flats*; Corsetten; *Hoops* [others have *Hoop*röcke, and *Hoopskirts* in neuer *Shapes*]; Haar Zöpfen; Rollen; *Braids*; *Puffs*; *Dress-Trimmings*. Unsere "*Fits*" sind vollkommen. *Yankee-Notions* [another has *Notionen*]. *Shelfing* und *Counter* für einen *Stohr*.

Pelzwaaren jeder Art, . . . Zobel; *Chinchilla*; *Ermin*; Siberien-*Squirrel*; *Fitch*; Wasser-*Mink*.

Wholesale und *Retail* Händler in Aechten *Rye Whiskeys* von verschiedenen *Bränden*, Ausländischen und Einheimischen *Brändies*, Weinen, *Gin* [G. Wachholderbranntwein], feiner Claret, *Scotch Ale*, *Fancy Liquors*, *Pine* Apfel Syrup, *Cherry* Wein und Kirschen *Brandy*, *Demijohns* und *Bottel*n von allen Gröszen.

Neue *Scale* Pianoes, mit eisernen Gestellen, *overstrung Base* und Agraffe *Bridge*. Ein schönes *Second Hand* Piano. Instrumenten zu groszen *Bärgen* . . . *Rotary Valve*[1] und *Side Action*[1] Instrumente [wind instruments].

Eisen-*Store* [Eisen-*Stohr*, Hartewaaren, *Hardwaaren*, Eisenwaaren] Küchen *Ränges*; Extra *Grätes*; *Furnäces*; *Bar-Room*-Oefen; *Air-Tight* und alle Sorten *Parlor* Oefen; *Heating*-Oefen [also Heiz-Oefen]; *Brilliant* Gas *Burner*; tragbare *Heaters*, und Gasbrenner; *Feuer-bricks*; Springs; *g*eforged und gerolltes eisen; *Schäfling*; *Safes*; Meisel [properly meiszeln] in *Setts*; *Razor Straps* und *Hones*; *pullys*; *Carving*messer, *Butcher*messer; *Varnisch* [for Firniss]; Neues Kohlen*screen*; *Boiler* von allen Sorten; *Brass*arbeit; Kaffeemühlen . . . verschiedene Haushaltgeräthschaften . . . . welche *Retail* oder *Wholesale* zu den billigsten Preisen verkauft werden . . . Sie garantiren völlige Satisfaction.

Porzellan-Waaren *Stohr*: *Queens*waaren; *Dinner Sets*; *Toilet Sets*; *Toy Thee Sets*; *Chamber Sets*; Schüszeln mit Deckel; *Bowl*en (Bowls) aller Arten; *Pitchers* aller Arten; Suppen *Tureens* . . . all die letzten *Styles* [Styl is also in use]. Ein groszer Vorrath *Waiters* und Thee-*Trays* . . . Haus-*Furnisching* Waaren . . . Vasen . . . *Chimney Tops*.

[1] These four words are printed in Roman type.

Schuh*store*: *India-Rubber, Lasting* und *Button* Schuhe ; hoch *polisch Gaiters* für frauen . . . *Kid* Schuhe . . . *Schlippers.*

Juwellen, *Watschen* und Uhren auf Hand [also 'an Hand' for vorräthig]; *Watschen* in goldenen und silbernen *Cäsen* [another has *Repeating*-Taschenuhr, for Repetiruhr]; *Watschen*-ketten ; Damen goldene *Bräcelet Setts ; Studs ; Sleeve*knöpfe ; Messern [for Messer].

Möbel-Waarenlager : Auswahl aller Arten Möbel . . . *Bureaus* [also Burös, Buros, Büros] ; *Sideboards* [*Seidbord, Desk*] ; *Dining*-Tische ; *Lounges ; Settees ;* [also *Setties*] ; *Wardrobes* [also Garderobe-Artikel, and Kleiderschrank, the proper term]. *Cänesitz* Stühle ; Fenster-blenden [and *Blinds*] ; *What-Nots ;* Spiegel mit Gold-*Främs ; Spring*betten . . . . *Parlor, Chamber,* und Küchen Möbeln . . . und alle andern Artikel welche in Möbel-*Stohrs* zu finden sind.

Bauholzhof [others have *Lumber-yard* and Bretterhof] . . . Alle Sorten von Banholz wohl ge*seasonet* [also vollkommen ausgetrocknet]; *Wetterboarding ;* Weiss*pein* [for Fichte] und *Hemlock* [for Tanne] *Joists* und *Scäntling* [another has *Hardwood Skäntling*] jeder Grösze ; *Bill-Stuffs ; Fenz*stoffen [for pl. stoffe, others have *Fensing* and *Fens*pfosten] ; *Flooring* [also Flurbretter] ; *Panel Lumber ; Poplarboards* [also Pappel] ; *Pickets* [also *Pälings*, both for Pfähle] von allen längen.

Buchdruckerei . . . *Job* Schriften ; *Programms* ; *Circulars ; Tickets ;* Karten ; *Blänks ; Handbills ;* Pamphlete ; *Billheads ;* . . . an seinem alten *Stünd.*

Oeffentliche *Vendu* [and Vendue—" *Vendue Creier* und Auktionär."] . . . Eine Bauerie [also *Farm,* and *Plantasche*] zu verkaufen . . . 110 Acker, 70 ge*klart* [and ge*klärt*] gelegen in *Londonderry Taunschip, Lebanon* [often Libanon] *County,* an der Strasze führend vom Palmyra *Landing*-Platze nach der *Jonestaun Road,* grenzend an den *Lebanon Valley* Riegelweg [and Rigelweg—a verbal translation of Railway. Others have—"Es grenzt an die Libanon Valley *Rail Road,*" and "Libanon Thal Eisenbahn."] 2 meilen vom *Stockyard* [location for cattle]. Die Verbesserungen sind ein groszes *weddergebordet*es [Eng. weather-boarded; another has " *Främ* Haus wettergebordet"] *Främhaus* [*Frähm*scheuer, *Bank*scheuer, *Frame*-Arbeits*hop*] neu tapezirt [papered] . . . mit fünf Stuben auf dem zweiten *Floor ; Garret* [others have Dachstube, and Dachzimmer] Küche und Keller. Eine Cisterne [also *Cistern*] mit 33 *Hogsheads* ; Kohlen*bin* unter dem *pävement* . . . Eine Bau*lotte* [building lot of ground] 50 Fusz *front* [also— die *Front*e, and *front*irend.] Schmied*schap* [*Wagenschoppen*] ; Wagen*sched* [zwei Wagen*schäde*] mit *Cribs* [and Krippen, Welschkorn*krieb*, Korn*kribbe*, Korn*kribb*] ; *Log*scheuer [also Block-Wohnhaus, *Logfräme*haus, blöckernes Haus]; mit Stein *Basement* [another has " Stallhoch Steinmauer"—the height of the stables of stone].

Das Land ist vom besten *Gravel* [also *Gravel*-Land, *Flint,* Kalkstein, Kalchstein, Feuerstein], und unter guten *Fenzen* [and *Fensen,* alles unter *Fenz,* gut einge*fenzt*].—Laufendes Wasser geht durch den Scheuerhof [also Scheuer*yard*]. Es ist bequem zu Post*officen,* Kirchen, Schulen, Mühlen, *Stohres,* und Handwerkern.

Ein 6-jähriger brauner *Gaul* ; . . . ein junges *Bay*pferd ; ein *Sorrel*pferd ; ein *Fallingtop-Buggy ;* ein *Rockaway* ; ein *Spring*wagen [*huckster*wagen] ; ein *Stohr*wagen mit drei *Springs ;* eine *Sweep Power* Dreschmaschine ; eine *Set Stäge*geschirr ; *Yankie*geschirr ; *Front*geschirre [for horses in front]. Welschkornscheller [also Welschkornschäler, Welschkornscräper, Welschkornausmacher, handscheller]; Schneidbox; Wagenbox [and Wagenbody]; Molasses-Faktry; Mückengeschirre [Fliegen-Geschirre, Fliegennetze]; 1 Lot Hausen's [housings for horses]; Windmühle, [translation of windmill, for Kornschwinge]; 1 Sink [kitchen sink - bench]; Martingales; Checkleinen; Cirkel-Säge [another has Circularsäge] mit Främ und Sträp.

Einige Pflanzgrundbeeren von Prince Alberts Sorte.

CHAPTER VI.

Syntax.

The confusion of forms in the declension of German articles, pronouns, and adjectives, as given in print, is avoided in dialects, and on the upper Rhine all classes use the masculine nominative *der* for the accusative *den*, thus making a step towards rational grammar—the feminine *die* and the neuter *das* being equally nominative and accusative. According to Radlof, from Swisserland to Holland, on both sides of the Rhine, there is scarcely a locality where the nominative is distinguished from the accusative and the dative, and he cites as examples—" ich trinke rother Wein " (for *rothen*); " ich habe der Esel gesehen " (for *den Esel*); " ich sitze auf der Baum " (for *dem Baum*).[1] In PG. this *rother* for *rothen* is sometimes cut down to ' root,' the common PG. neuter form, particularly with the *definite* article, as in—

Ich trink d'r root wei,. *I drink the red wine.*

Was f'r wei, wit [willst du] trinke? *What kind of wine willst drink ?*

Ich trink tschenərli rooter wei,.[1] *I 'generally' drink red wine.*

---

[1] . . . " Von der Schweiz an zu beiden seiten des Rheines hinab bis an Hollands gränzen, giebt es kaum einige Gegenden, wo man den Koch vom Kellner, den Herrn vom Knechte, den Hammer vom Amboſze, d.i. den Werfall (*Nominativ*) vom Wenfalle (*Accusativ*) und dem Wemfalle (*Dativ*) richtig zu unterscheiden vermöchte. Bald hört man nehmlich : " ich trinke rother Wein " bald : " ich habe der Esel gesehen " bald : " ich sitze auf der Baum." s.f."—*Dr. Joh. Gottl. Radlof, Mustersaal aller teutschen Mund-arten*, . . . Bonn, 1822 ; 2, 90.

Stalder (Schweiz. Idiotikon, 1812) gives the accusatives of *der* and *ein* as agreeing with the nominative, and under *ein* (1, 37) he has—Acc. wie der Nom., welches überhaupt zu bemerken ist.

[When I read extracts from this Treatise before the Philological Society on 3 June, 1870, Prof. Goldstücker and Dr. E. Mall, the latter an Alsatian, both considered that this presumed substitution of the nominative for the accusative or dative case must be a misapprehension. Dr. Mall declared himself totally unaware of it. Both considered that it must have resulted from the disappearance of the inflectional -*m*, -*n* (the latter of which is the rule certainly in the Rhine region), and the degradation of the preceding *e* vowel into *ə*. This would account for " ich trinke rother Wein," considering *rother* to mean ' roots,' but would not account for " ich habe der Esel gesehen," in which the *r* must be taken as trilled, unless we consider that first *den* was made into ' də,' and then the ' r ' *evolved* as in the Cockney's ' idea-r of things.' Hence the original passages on which the assertions in the text are founded, have been added.—*Alex. J. Ellis.*]

G. Wir geben guten Lohn. PG. M'r gewwə guutər loo,. *We give good wages.*
.ən guutər freind (n guuti fraa, n guut haus) is n guut ding. *A good friend*
(masc.), *wife* (fem.), *house* (neut.) *is a good thing* (neut.).
Sellər mann hət mei, huut alles ufgebrəchə. *That man has broken* (meinen)
my hat (alles auf) *all up.*

Ich bin naus in də r hoof un bin unsərər kats uf də r schwants getrettə,
selli hət mich gekratst. (*Nsp.*) *I went* (hinaus) *out, in* (G. den Hof, *m.*) *the
yard, and trod on* (G. den Schwanz) *the tail of our cat, she scratched me.*

. . . weil ich mich geschämmt hab, bin ich uf də r schpeichər geschniikt
oonə ən wərt tsu saaghə. (*Nsp.*) *While I shamed myself, I ' sneaked' up to* (den)
the loft without a word to say.

G. Das Wetter ist den ganzen Tag schön gewesen. PG. s wettor iss d'r gants
(or gans) daak schee, gwest. *The weather has been fine the entire day.*

G. Ich gehə in den Keller. PG. Ich gee in dər kellər. *I am going into the
cellar.*

In the next, *Stuhl* being masculine, the nominative *der* is
used for the dative *dem*, but the accusative *ihn* ('n) is preserved—

ær hət uf d'r schtuul k'həkt, un hət n f'rbrəchə. *He sat on the chair and has
broken it.*

G. Liebe deinen Nächsten, als dich selbst. *Love thy neighbor as thyself.*
PG. Liib dei, nochbər ass wii dich selwər.

G. Lēgĕ das Buch auf dēn Tisch. *Lay the book on the table.* PG. Leeg s
buch uf d'r tisch.

Here, if ' den tisch ' were used in PG. it would rather mean
this table,' because there is a tendency to use articles as
demonstratives, saying ' dœr ' for G. *dieser*, and ' sellər ' (G.
selbiger) for G. *jener*,—' sel ' (G. selbiges) being its neuter, and
' selli ' (G. selbige) its feminine and plural. This ' sel ' is
found in Swisserland, and other parts of the Rhine region.
Its Alsatian form *tsel*, with initial *t*, shows that it is akin to
G. *dasselbe*. Notwithstanding its resemblance in form and
function to Provensal *sel* or *cel*, French *celui, celle*, they are
without etymologic relation. See Ch. VII., § 2. p. 43, and § 4,
p. 45 ; and *Ellis*, Early English Pronunciation, p. 662, note 15.

' Das' (the) and ' es' (it) have a tendency to confusion under
the short form 's used for both. ' Dass ' (that) remains, and

---

1 " Dii Jarik Kaunti leit, wann sii fum rootə wei, schwätzə, saaghə g'weenlich
—"Ich trink rootər wei,." Wann sii awər kee rootər hen, dann trinkə sii
weisser wann sii n kriighə kennə." *The Rev. D. Ziegler*, letter of Jan. 16, 1870
(literatim).

the neuter nominative article is changed from G. *das* to PG.
'des,' as in 'des buch' (the book)—but as 'des buch' may
mean *this book*, the function of the article is performed by
reducing this 'des' to 's, as in—

.s buch iss mei, *the book is mine*—des buch iss mei, THIS *book is mine.*

"Donn hab ich gedenkt [not *gedacht*], d e s is doch now ordlich plain
deitsch," . . . (*Rauch.*[1]) *Then I thought,* THIS *is at-any-rate 'now' tolerably
'plain' Dutch.*

Dær mann iss krankər (not *kränker*) wie d'r annər. THIS *man is sicker than
the other.* (G. als der andere.)

G. Ein Mann und eine Frau waren hier diesen Morgen. *A man and a woman
were here this morning.* PG. Es war ən mann un ən fraa hiir den mårighə.
There was a man and a woman here this morning.

G. Ich wünsche dass er komme. *I wish that he come.* PG. Ich wətt (or
wott, for *wollte*) dass ær deet [G. thät] kummə. *I would that he would come.*
Swiss—I wett, asz er chäm. *Stalder,* 1, 112.

Swiss *asz* for *dass* is often used in PG., as in—

Wann ich geglaabt hätt 'ass er mich net betsaalt (or betsaalə deet), so hätt
ich 'm gar net gebárikt (or gebaricht). *If I had believed that he would not pay
me, I would* (gar nicht) *not at all have* (geborgt) *trusted him.*

Wann ich gedenkt [not G. *gedacht*] hätt 'ass es net woor wæær, dann hätt ich
's net geglaabt. *If I had not supposed it to be true, I would not have* (geglaubt)
believed it.

G. Wäre er reich, er würde nicht betteln. *Were he rich he would not beg.*
G. Wenn er reich wäre, so würde er nicht betteln. PG. Wann ær reich wæær,
deet ær net bettəln. *If he were rich, he would not beg.*

PG., like Swiss,[2] dislikes the imperfect tense, and prefers
G. *Ich habe gedacht* (I have thought), to G. *Ich dachte* (I
thought), which gives forms like—

Wii ich n gesee, hab, hab ich gedenkt ær wært k'sund. *As I saw him* (having
seen him) *I thought he would get well.*
Ich bin gangə *I have gone ;* not G. Ich gieng *I went,* nor gegangen *ygone.*

Whan myn houfbond is fro the world i-gon,—*Chaucer,* (*Wright's ed.*) 1. 5629.
With menftralcy and noyfe that was (y-)maked, 1. 2526.
Bet is to be (y-)weddid than to brynne. 1. 5634.

PG. has also 'kummə' (has come) for G. gekommen, show-
ing a tendency to follow a law which caused ge- (y-, i-) to be
dropped in English. The practice seems to have started with

[1] In a spelling based upon English, and not fully phonetic. See *Ellis,* Early
English Pronunciation, pp. 654-661.
[2] *Stalder* (1, 46) says that the imperfects war, hatte, sagte, kam, rufte, kaufte,
would be scarcely understood in Swisserland.

gekommen and *gegangen*, because they are much used, and
their initial guttural absorbs the guttural *g-* or *k-* of the prefix.
In an Austrian dialect,[1] *ge-* disappears before *b, p, d, t, z,* as
in "Ih bin kumma" (I have come), PG. Ich bin kumnə.

PG. Ich hab s [G. gekauft] kaaft im schtoor. *I bought it at the 'store.'*
Həscht mei, briif krikt? *Hast* (G. gekriegt) *received my letter?* Ich schreib n
briif. *I write a letter.*

"Der Charle hat jung geheiert un   D'r 'Tschœrli' hət jung k'eiərt un
hat ə fleiszige Fra krickt," *Wollen-*   hət ə fleissighə fraa krikt.
weber, p. 78.

'Charley' married young and got an industrious wife.

G. Es regne. *It may rain.* PG. s maak (G. mag) reeghərə.
G. Es regnete. *It might rain.* PG. s kennt (G. könnt) reeghərə.
G. Es habe geregnet. *It may have rained.* PG. s kennt reeghə hawwə.

PG. has the Swiss *als* (hitherto, formerly, always), a form
in which it is not shortened into *a's,* as in—

œr hət als ksaat œr wœr (or wæœr) miir niks schuldich. (*Ziegler*). *He has
hitherto said he is to-me nothing indebted.*

Mr. Rauch, in his partly English spelling, has—

"Er hut aw behawpt das mer set   .œr hət aa behaapt dass mər set
sich net rula lussə bi seiner fraw,   sich net 'ruulə' lossə bei seinər fraa,
un das de weiver nix wissa fun   un dass dii weiwər niks wissə fun
denna sacha, un das es kens fun earn   dennə sachə, un dass es kens fun eerə
bisness is we an monn vote odder   'bissnəss' iss wii ən mann 'woot,' ədər
we oft er als drinkt."   wii əft œr als drinkt.

He (has) maintained that one should not (lassen) *let* (sich) *one's-self be 'ruled'
by one's wife, and that the* (weiber nichts wissen) *women know nothing of such
things, and that it is* (keines von ihre) *none of their 'business' how a man 'votes,'
or how oft he* (als) ALWAYS *drinks.*

In the following Suabian example (Radlof 2, 17) *als* is a
form of G. alles (all), and *schmieren* is used as in PG. for *to
pay off, to trick.*

Kurz! i will olls eba macha   In short, I will make all so even
Daſz oim 's Herz im Leib mu'ſz lacha; that the heart in one's body must laugh;
I will au de Tuifel ſchmiera,   I will also trick [den] the devil
Daſz er Niemʌ kan verführa,   that he none can lead astray—
Hack' ihm boyde Hörner o,   chop for him both his horns off
Daſz er nimma ſtecha ka-.   that he cannot thrust again.

PG. 'dass' for *als* (with the sense of *as*), and 'dass wan'
G. als *wenn* (South German of Breisgau *as wenn*) for *as if*,
seems peculiar. The German adverbial particles admit of a

[1] *Castelli,* Wörterbuch, Wien, 1847, p. 30.

wide range of meaning, and in Low Austrian certain inversions occur, as *aussa* (aus-her) for G. *heraus; aussi* (àus-hin), also in old Bavarian, for G. *hinaus*, which would allow PG. 'dass' to be referred to *als dasz* or da(r)als.[1] But independently of this surmise, the cutting down of the pronouns *des* (G. das) and *es* to 's, and *als* to *ass*, makes it as easy to accept *dass* for *als*, as 'd of English 'I 'd rather,' for *had* instead of *would*. Farther, as *da* has *als* for one of its meanings, this *dass* may be *da* with the adverbial suffix -*s*.[2]

' des land is aw frei for mich so goot das for dich."—*Rauch*, p. 32.	. . . des land is aa frei f'r mich soo guut dass f'r dich.

This (not *the*) *country is* (auch) *also free for me as well* AS *for thee.*

" net wennicher dos sivva hunnert for dich un mich" . . .—*Rauch*, 1869.	. . . net wennichər dass siwə hunərt f'r dich un mich.

Not less THAN *seven hundred for thee and me.*

"Er will hawa dos ich bei eam aw roof in Filldelfy, un dut d o s w a n n s tsu meiner advantage wær wann ich kumm."—*Rauch*, Aug. 16, '69.	.ær will hawə dass ich bei iim aa,ruuf in Fildelfi, un duut dass wann s tsu meinər 'atfæntitsch' wær wann ich kumm.

He will have that I (bei) *at-the-house-of him* [G. *anrufen*, perverted to an English idiom] *call-on in Phildelphi* [the common pronunciation] *and* (*he*) *does* AS IF *it* (were) *would be to my ' advantage ' if I come.*[3]

" Selly froke hut mich awer sheer gorly schwitza macha, un ich hob g'feeld yusht. grawd d a s w a n n ich mich full heaser hulder tæ g'suffa het un g'mixd mit tansy, katzakraut un bebbcrmint."—*Rauch*, Aug. 9, 1869.	Selli frook hət mich sch'ir gaarli schwitsə machə, und ich hab kf'iilt jascht graad dass wann ich mich fəl heesər huldər tee ksəffə het un 'gmikst' mit 'tœnsi' [s not as z] katsəkraut un ' bebbərmint.'

[Dieselbe Frage] *That question however almost* [G. gar] *quite made me sweat, and I felt just exactly* AS IF *I had* (G. gesoffen) *drunk myself full of hot* (G. Holder) *elder tea, and ' mixed ' with ' tansy ' catnip and ' peppermint.'*

" 's scheint m'r wærklich a s w a n n du im sinn hätscht in deinə altə daaghə noch n Dichter tsu gewə (tsu wærrə). Awər ich færricht 's iss tsu schpot; du hätscht ə paar joor friiər aa,fange sollə, danx wær viileicht ebbəs draus [G. worden] warrə."[4] *It appears to me really* AS IF *you intended in your old days yet to become a poet. But I fear it is too late ; you should have commenced a few years earlier, then perhaps something might have come of it.*

---

[1] Suabian condenses *da unten* to *dunda*. The Rev. D. Ziegler suggests that this ' dass ' may have arisen from a *d*, as of ' grad ' (G. gerade) before ' as ' of *als*, as in—ær schwätzt grad *as* wann [G. wenn] ær reich wær. (He speaks just as if he were rich.) [2] See *Hald.* Affixes. p. 213.

[3] The present tense (' wann ich kumm') is used here for the G. subjunctive *wenn ich käme.*

[4] The Rev. D. Ziegler, transliterated by himself.

The next is from the description of a willow-tree with the
'nesht' (pl. of G. *nast*[1]) branches broken by ice.[2]

"Er guckt net gans so stattlich meh,   .ær gukt net gans soo schtattlich mee
Er guckt net gans so gross un' schoe   ær gukt net gans soo gross un schee,
D a s wie er hut die anner woch   dass wii ær hət dil anər woch
Wu'r all sei nesht hut katte noch."   wuu 'r all sei, noscht hət kattə noch.

It (nicht mehr) *no more looks quite so stately, it looks not* (ganz) *quite so large
and fine,* AS THAT *it did the* (andere) *other week,* (wo er *where he*) *when it* (hat
gehabt) *has had all its boughs.*

At present PG. is exhibiting a tendency to drop G. *su* (to),
the sign of the so-called infinitive, altho in the following examples perhaps most speakers would use it.

Wann fangscht aa, [tsu] schaffə?   *When do you begin* [to] *work ?*
Ich hab aa fangə schaffə.   *I have begun* (*to*) *work.*
. . . fiil annəri hen hart prowürt sich farnə naus schaffə.   (*Rauch.*)
Many others (have) *tried hard* (to) *work themselves* (G. vorn) *forward.*

[1] The usual German is *ast*, pl. *äste*. Schmeller (*Mundarten Bayerns*, art. 610)
notices the following examples of this initial *n* in Bavarian dialects; his pho-
netical spelling is given in italics, and interpreted into the present in brackets:
der *Nä'n* [Noon] 'A'then: *Näst* [nost] Ast; die Näf'n [noozn] 'A'sen; *Nassʹl*
[nassl] Assel; *Närb* [nɑrb] Arb; *Neichté* [neichte] Eichte; *Nuərəʹ* [Nuərə]
Urhab; *Nuesch* [Nuesch] Uesch. In art. 545 he also gives the form ə *Luesch,*
and in art. 636, the form əʹʹ *Räufʹn,* for Uesch, a gutter, and 'A'sen, a beam or
joist. *Närb* is the staple on the door, which carries the padlock; *Eicht* is a little
while. The following are examples of omitted initial *n*, (ib. art. 611); *dər
'Apoleon* Napoleon; *'idəʹ* nider, *'Ankinet* Nanquinet; *'Impfəʹʹburg* Nymphen-
burg; ganz *'atürliʹ* natürlich; *'ében, 'iəbn* neben; *'achər, 'achəʹ* nachher; *'Eʹst,
'iəft* Nest. St. Antwein und St. Nantwein, Aventin Chron. Edit. v. 1566, fol.
470.—Compare the English added initial *n* in *nickname* (nckename for ekename,
see Pr. Parv.), *niggot, nugget* for ingot; *newt* for eft, ewt; *nawl* for awl; *nunkle*
for uncle; *Nan, Ned, Noll,* for Anne, Edward, Oliver:—and the omitted initial
n in *adder* (old edres and neddres), *apron* for napron, *eyas* for nias.—*A. J. Ellis.*

[2] Poems. By Rachel Bahn. York, Pa. 1869. Containing twenty pages of
"Poems in Pennsylvania Dutch." Noticed by me in Trübner's *American and
Oriental Literary Record*, Jan. 24, 1870, p. 634. The following may be con-
sulted also:
Gemälde aus dem Pennsylvanichen Volksleben . . . . von L. A. Wollenweber.
Philadelphia und Leipzig. Schäfer und Koradi, 1869.
Harbaugh's Harfe. Gedichte in Pennsylvanisch-Deutscher Mundart. Phila-
delphia, Reformed Church Publication Board, 1870.
On the German Vernacular of Pennsylvania. By S. S. Haldeman. Trans.
Am. Philological Association, 1869-70.
Lancaster Pa. WEEKLY ENTERPRISE (newspaper), with a weekly article by
Mr. Rauch.
Der Waffenlose Wächter (monthly newspaper). Gap P.O., Lancaster Co. Pa.
Early English Pronunciation, . . . by Alexander J. Ellis, F.R.S., F.S.A.
London, 1871. Twelve pages (652-65) are devoted to Pennsylvania German.
P'älzische G'schichtə' . . . von Franz von Kobell. München, 1863. In the
main, this little volume of 'Palatinate Stories' comes nearer to Pennsylvania
German than any other I have seen.

"De mæd . . . hen kea so kleany
bonnets g'hat di nix sin for hitz
odder kelt ; es wara rechtshaffene
bonnets, das mer aw sea hut kenne
ohna de brill uf du."—*Nsp.*

Dü meed hen kee, soo klee,ni
'bannəts' katt dii niks sin f'r hits
əd'r kelt ; es waarə rechtschaffənə
'bannəts,' dass m'r aa seeə hət kennə,
oone dii brill uf [tsu] duu,.

The girls (haben gehabt) *had no such small ' bonnets'* (die) *which are nothing
for heat or* (kälte) *cold ; there were honest ' bonnets' that* (mir) *one* (auch) *also
could see without putting the spectacles on.*

PG. Sometimes distinguishes between the present tense and
the aorist, as in Swiss—" er thuot choh " (he does come)—

Sellər hund knarrt.   *That dog growls* (has a habit of growling).
Sellər hund tuut (G. thut) knarrə.   *That dog is now growling.*
D'r mann tuut essə—ær iss am essə.   *The man is eating—he is at eating.*

PG. does not use equivalents to *neither* and *nor.*

G. Er ist *weder* reich *noch* arm.   *He is neither rich nor poor.*   PG. ær iss net
reich un net aarm.

E. He is *either* sick *or* lazy.   PG. ær iss krank ədər faul.   (Or, adopting
either and its idiom) ær iss ' iitər' krank ədər faul.

In a case like the last, no matter how well the speaker
knows English, he must *not* pronounce a word like ' either '
in the English mode, because it would be an offense against
the natural rhetoric of the dialect.

CHAPTER VII.

Comparisons with other Dialects.

§ 1. PG. *not Swiss.*

PG. is not Swiss, altho it has a number of Swiss charac-
teristics, and the line (Radlof, 2, 68)—

"Was isch säll für e sufere kärli?"

is very near its PG. form—

Was isch sel f'r o saubor kœrli? *What sort of cleanly fellow is that?*

PG. has both ' ær iss ' and ' ær isch ' (he is) according to
the locality, of which the latter may be less common. The
Rev. D. Ziegler (a native, like myself) refers the ' isch ' variety
to the Mennonite and Dunker population, and as there were
many Dunkers (or Tunkers) where my early years were passed,
I heard more of this than of the other.

The indicative mood present tense of *haben* and *sein* are,
with some variations, as follows (Stalder, 1, 47–50)—

Swiss.	PG.	Swiss.	PG.
i hah ;	ich hab, hap, *I have.*	i bi ;	ich bin, *I am.*
de hest ;	du hascht, *thou hast.*	de bisch, bist ;	du bischt, *thou art.*
er hed, hett ;	œr hot, *he has.*	er isch, ist ;	œr iss, isch, *he is.*
mer hend ;	m'r hen, *we have.*	mer sind ;	m'r sin, *we are.*
der hend ;	d'r hent, *you have.*	der sind ;	d'r sint, *you are.*
sj hend ;	sii hen, *they have.*	sj sind ;	sii sin, *they are.*

Here the dative singular *mir* (to me) is used in the nominative plural instead of *wir* (we), and also in impersonal expressions ; and the dative singular *dir* (to thee) is similarly used
for *Ihr* (you), as in 'd'r sint' for G. *Ihr seid* (you are). G.
Ihr habet (you have) has forced its *t* upon the first and third
persons plural of the Swiss forms ; and in PG. the second
person is sometimes forced upon the third, as in the following,
from the Wollenweber's Gemälde (in the German character),
1869, p. 124,—

For äbout 32 Johr z'rick,	'Fr ebaut' tswee-un-dreissich joor tsrik,
do h e n t unsre ... Schaffleut	do hent unsre ... schaffleit ...
...im Stenbruch geschafft, un sten	im schtee,bruch geschafft, un schtee,
gebroche, for de grosze Damm zu	gebrocho f'r di grosse 'damm' tsu fixe.
fixe.	

'*For about*' *thirty-two years back, here have our laborers worked in the quarry,
and quarried stone to* '*fix*' *the big* '*dam*.' (Here the English *fix* and *dam* are
used, instead of G. *fixiren*, and *der damm*.)

Here the first *for* may be regarded as English, but the
second occurs in the Palatinate—"for den Herr Ring sehr
ungünschtig" (Kobell), *for Mr. Ring very unfavorable*—"for
sei Lügerei,"—*for his truthlessness.*

The next is extracted from a poem by Tobias Witmer, dated
from the State of New York, June 1, 1869, printed in the
'Father Abraham' English newspaper, in roman type, and
reprinted Feb. 18, 1870. The original spelling is that of Mr.
Rauch, and is not reproduced. Dialectic words are s p a c e d,
and English words are here put in *italics*. The translation is
rather free.

Geburts-Daak—An mei, Alti.	Birthday—To my Wife.
Oo wass is schenner uf der welt	Oh what is finer in the world
d a s s blimlin, root un weiss ?	than flowrets red and white ?
un bloo un g e e l,[1] im ærblo [2] felt	and blue and yellow in the field
wass sin sii doch so *neis* !	how beautiful and bright.
Ich wees noch guut, in s e l l e r tseit	I know yet well that in that time,
hab ich niks lüwers duu,[3]	nought would I rather do,
d a s s in dii wisso—lang un breit	than in the meadows long and wide
so blimlin ksuucht wii duu.	such flowrets seek as you.
Doch iss es schun o lang-i tseit	Yet it is quite a lengthened time,
sid'r ich dart in dem felt,	since I in yonder field,
dii blimlin ksuucht, uf lang un breit,	sought out the flowers far and wide,
un uf dei, *bussom* k s c h p e l l t .	and on thy bosom pinned.
D' r h e n t emool o gærtl kat—	You also had a garden bed—
mei, schwesterli un duu ; [schpaat	you and my sister fair,
ich hab s *pripeerd* · mit hak un	which I prepared with hoe and spade
dii blummo nei, tsu duu, ;	to set the flowers there ;
un wuu ich hab im grossi s c h w e e l,	and where I in the ample vale [4]
dii kii dart h i n n o ksuucht,	the cattle there had sought,

[1] G. gelb, Ohg. gelo, Swiss, etc., gäl *yellow.*
[2] Not PG. ærpso, G. erbsen (peas), but a form of *erdbeere* (strawberry).
[3] G. Ich habe nichts lieber gethan. (G. adj. and adv. *lieber*, adverbialised
with *-s*.) *Nothing would I rather have done.*
[4] The word is "schwœhl" in the original—probably borrowed from the local
English word *swale*. Wuu, G. wo, *where*. The author was born in 1816, at
Niagara, in a small colony which had emigrated from Lancaster county, Pennsylvania—his father in 1811. The colony received additions about the year 1830.

dii *leedi-schlipparss*, weiss un g e e l,
hab ich mit, heem gebracht,
un hab sii in s e l gœrtl plantst
bei nacht, in muundəs licht : [*wantst* [1]
d'r h e n t s nct gwist, bis juscht *æt*
h e n t dür s go*gest* s war mich.

the lady-slippers, gold, and pale,
with me I homeward brought,
and in that garden bed at night
I set them when the moon was light.
You did not know who it could be,
but all at once you thought of me.

§ 2. PG. *not Bavarian.*

PG., Bavarian, Austrian and Suabian have the vowel of
fall, and nasal vowels. In Pangkofer's *Gedichte in Altbayer-
ischer Mundart*, are the PG. words 'aa' *also* ; 'bissel' *a little* ;
'ebbas,' G. etwas *something* ; 'do is' *there is* ; 'glei' (also
Austrian) *soon* ; 'sunst,' G. sonst *besides* ; 'frumm,' G. fromm
kind ; 'kloo' *claw* ; 'kumma,' G. gekommen *come* ; Ohg.
'coman' and 'cuman' *to come* ; 'mir' *we*, for G. wir ; 'sel,' G.
dasselbe *that-same* ; but PG. has not 'mi' *me* ; 'di' *thee* ;
'hoarn' *horn* ; 'hout' *has* ; 'thuan' *to do* ; 'g'spoasz,' *sport* ;
'oamal' *once* ; 'zwoa' *two*, G. zwei, PG. 'tswee'; wei, PG.
'weip' *wife* ; zon, PG. 'tsum' *to the.*

The following example of upper Bavarian is given by Klein,[2]
beside which a PG. version is placed for comparison.

" Schau, nachbe', wàs mei' freud' is,—
In suntàe', in der frûe,
Gorn lûs' i' in mei'n gâârt'l
'n kircheläut'n zue.

Sii nochbər wass mei, frcet iss !
Am sundaak marrgbə frii,
Gœrn hœær [3] ich in mei, m gœrtli
Dii kærchə-*bella* hii,.[4]

" Dà is 's so still und hâemli',
Kâe' lärm, kâe g'schrâc kimmt 'nei' :
In'n himmi kà's nit schöner
W' as in mei'n gâârt'l sci'."

Do 's iss so schtill un heemlich,
Kee, jacht, kee, kschrci kummt nei, ;
Jm himml kann s nct schee,nər
Wii s in mei,m gœrtl sci.

See neighbor, what my joy is, on Sunday in the morn ; I listen in my garden,
to the church-bell ring. Here it is so still and calm, no turmoil, no strife comes
within ; in heaven (kann es nicht) it cannot be fairer than (es) it is in my little
garden.

---

[1] = *at once.* Dr. Jones, 1701, gives '*wœns, wœnst*' as the English pronunciation in Shropshire and some parts of Wales. Buchanan, 1766, gives '*wœns*'
as correct English.—*A. J. Ellis.*
[2] Die Sprache der Luxemburger. Luxemburg, 1855.
[3] This word varies to hecr, and horch may be used.
[4] Here *hii*, is given for the rhyme, the proper word being G. *da*, PG. 'doo.'
On this account the Rev. D. Ziegler makes the following variation on my
version—
Sii noochbər was mei, frcet iss,
Wann ich im gœrtli schtce,
Gœrn heer ich frii am sundaak
Dii kærchəbcllə geh.

§ 3. PG. *not Suabian.*

The Pennsylvania Germans have traditional stories against the Suabians, although their population is in part derived from the upper (Pfalz) Palatinate; and some Suabians settled in Northumberland County, Pa., the evidence of which remains in the name of a stream, *Schwaben* (or *Swope*) Creek.

PG. resembles Suabian in using ' e, ee' for *ö*, and 'ii' for *ü*—in the loss of infinitive -*n*,—in turning final -*n* into a nasal vowel (as in sei₋ for *seyn*), and in saying ' du bischt,' ' du kannscht,' etc. (for G. *du bist*), 'du witt' for *du willst;* 'nimme' for *nicht mehr;* 'glei' for *gleich* in the sense of *soon* —but the adjective 'gleich' (similar) remains. PG. does not turn *o* into *au*, as in Suabian '*braut*,' '*hauch*,' for *brot, hoch;* nor cut down G. *ich habe* to '*i ha*'; it does not add elements, as in '*bois*' for G. *bös*, PG. ' bees,' '*bluat*' for G. *blut*, '*reacht*' for *recht*, '*kuine*' for *keine*, and '*stuinige fealder*' for *steinige felder*, a peculiarity of Suabian, Alsatian, Swiss, Bavarian and its kin Austrian. PG. has archaic 'hees' (hot) for G. *heisz*, but nothing like Bavarian *haəs.*

Difference of pronunciation causes confusion of speech between speakers of different dialects, as shown by Dr. Rapp in his Physiologie der Sprache, 4, 131. In the 'Fliegende Blätter' (13, 158) there is a dialogue called 'Ein Deutsch-Böhme' (a German Bohemian), between a *Bauer* and a *Städter*—but a Swiss speaker is now added, with the rejoinder to his remark.

Bauer. Wie is de Suppe so häsz!
Städter. Man sagt ja nicht hāsz, sondern heisz. Has [G. hase, PG. haas *hare*] nennt man das Thier. . . .
Bauer. Dōs hāszt bei uns Hōs!
Städter. Das ist wieder falsch. Hōs bedeutet jenes Kleidungsstück, womit Eure langen Beine bedeckt sind.
Bauer. Dös hāszt Hus!
Schweitzer. Aber mer sind jets im Huus.
Bauer. Dös iss 'n *Haus!*

Diminutives in PG. and Suabian are made with -li; both use ' des' for *das*, ' uffm' for *auf dem*, ' biirə' for *birnen*, ' g'hat' or 'kat' for *gehabt*, 'suu₋' for *sohn*, 'schoof' for *schâf*, 'Schwop' for *Schwâbe*, ' als ' for *alles*, and ' as' for *als*.

§ 4. PG. *not Alsatian*.

In the very German county of Berks there is an Elsass township, which indicates an Alsatian influence. As a German province of France,[1] two languages are in use, and are taught in the schools, but the French is Germanised in pronunciation, as may be verified among the Alsatian and German servants of Paris. Being akin to Swiss and Suabian, PG. has some points in common with this dialect, without being influenced by French.

Alsatian differs from PG. in having *i haa* for 'ich hab,' *tsel* for 'sel' (G. *dersel*be), *bluət* for 'bluut,' *üss* for 'aus,' *hüs* for 'haus,' *tsiit* for 'tseit,' *bisch* for 'bischt,' *biim* for 'bei'm,' *morje* for 'marrghə.'

PG. and Alsatian turn some *b*-s to *w*, they have the vowels of *fall, what, up*, and have 'prowiirə' for *probiren*, 'ass' for *als*, 'do' for *da*, 'joo' for *ja*, 'joor' for *jahr*, 'hoor' for *haar*, 'fun' for *von*, 'isch' for *ist*, 'jets' for *jetzt*, 'uff' for *auf*, 'druff' for *dorauf*, 'uff'm' for *auf dem*, 'raus' for *daraus*, 'draan' for *daran*, 'iwwər' for *über*, 'dno' for *darnach;* PG. 'əffə,' Alsat. 'offə,' G. *ofen;* 'bal' for *bald*, 'm'r' for *wir*, 'm'r muss' for *man musz*, 'mœe' for *mehr*, 'welli' for *welche;* 'was batt s' (what boots it).

The following lines (Radlof, 2, 110) are extracted from a piece of Alsatian which well illustrates the concurrent use of two languages. The French should be read in the German mode. Other French words occur in Radlof's examples, such as allong *allons*, tur *tour*, schalu *jaloux*, anterpoo *entrepôt*, bangenet *baïonnette*. The original of the following is in German (gothic) and French (roman) print according to the lan-

---

[1] This was written before the Franco-German war which re-annexed Alsatia to Germany. When I read out the first example in Chapter VIII. (*Wüdər aa,geschmürt*), to the Philological Society, on communicating this paper, 3 June, 1870, Dr. E. Mall, an Alsatian, who was present, remarked that it reminded him throughout of his native dialect, of which he thoroughly recognized the pronunciation. I may remark that I have never heard PG. pronounced, although I have heard Austrian, Saxon, Rhenish, Bavarian, and Swiss dialects, and read solely by the phonetic orthography here given.—*A. J. Ellis.*

guage, here imitated by roman and italic types. The speaker
is telling a friend how she was addressed by a stranger :

> So kummt ä Wälscher her, und macht mit Kumblemente,
> Und redt mich gradzu an.—Mach er kein Spargemente,[1]
> Hab i glich zu ihm g'sait. Losz Er, was ich 'ne bitt,
> Mich mine Waih fortgehn ; ich kenn de Herre nit.
> *,,Sans avoir,* frout er mich, *l'honneur de vous connaître,*
> *,,Vous êtes seule ici, voulez-vous me permettre*
> *,,De vous offrir mon bras pour vous accompagner ?*
> *Allez, Mousié,* sa ich, *allez-vous promener,*
> Und spar Er sich die müh ; Er musz sich nit trumpire,
> Ich bin von dene nit die mer am Arm kann führe.[2]
> *,,Vous êtes bien cruelle,* arrêtez un moment,
> Sait er, und kummt soglich mit sine Santimang. . . .
> Zu diene, hab i g'sait ; losz Er mich aber gehn,
> Min Ehr erlaubt mir nit noch länger do zu stehn.
> *,,Je n'insisterai pas, mais veuillez bien m'apprendre,*
> *,,Si demain en ces lieux vous daignerez vous rendre.*
> Behüt mich Gott davor ! i gib kein *rendez-vus.*
> *Adié, mousié, adié, je ne vus* [sic] *verrai plus.*

Translation.—Thus comes a Frenchman up and proceeds with compliments,
and (an-redet) accosts me (gerade zu) directly. Make no formalities,[1] I said
to him at once. Let me, what I beg ('ne, G. ihn) him, continue (meinen weg)
my way—I know not the (herren) gentlemen. *" Without having,"* he (frägt)
asked me, *" the honor of knowing you, you are alone here, will you permit me to
offer you my arm to accompany you ?"* Go, sir, (sagte) said I, *Proceed with your
walk*—and spare himself the trouble ; he must not deceive himself, I am not of
those who can be conducted on the arm.[2] *" You are very cruel, stay a moment,"*
says he—and comes at once with his sentiment. . . . At your service, I said,
he should let me go, my honor would not allow me to stand there longer. *" I
do not insist, but will you kindly inform me, if to-morrow in these places you will
deign to return."* Preserve me heaven from it ! I give no *rendez-vous* ; adieu,
sir, adieu, I will not see you more.

§ 5. PG. *is akin to several South German Dialects.*

Like *Suabia,* the name of *Pfalz* has disappeared from the
map of Europe, and what was once the Lower Palatinate, is
now to be looked for chiefly in Baden, Bavaria, and Darmstadt.

---

[1] F. E. Petri (Handbuch der Fremdwörter, 1845) explains *Spargimént* or
Spargemént as "ein ausgestreutes Gerücht, Ausgesprenge, Geträtsch oder Gerede ;
Aussprengsel," in short, *gossip* or *idle talk*, evidently from Latin *spargere.*—
A. J. Ellis.

[2] Compare Goethe's *Faust* —
> *Faust.*   Mein schönes Fräulein, darf ich wagen,
>   Meinen Arm und Geleit Ihr anzutragen ?
> *Margarete.*   Bin weder Fräulein, weder schön,
>   Kann ungeleitet nach Hause gehn.—*A. J. E.*

It was partly bounded by Alsatia, Baden, and Würtemberg, and Manheim was the chief city. A few examples, condensed from Kobel, will show the nearness of its dialect to PG.

So nehmt er dann desz Album desz uff 'm Tisch gelege is. *So takes he then the album that is laid on the table.* So is 'm glei' ei'gfalle'. *So it soon happened to him.* Guck emol, do is er, mer kennt 'n. *Look once, here he is, one knows him.* Wei is er dann do drzu kumme? *How then has he come?* Desz will ich Ihne sage. *That I will tell you.* Mer hot nix mehr vun 'm g'hört. *Nothing more has been heard of him.* Mir habe [PG. mr hen] alls minanner 'gesse. *We ate all together.* Juscht am selle Tag is e' Gascht a'kumme. *Precisely on that day a guest arrived.* Mit eme finschtre' Gesicht. *With a dark face.* Sacha macha for die Leut. *To make things for people.* Bsunners *especially;* ghat had; drbei *thereby;* schun *already;* sunscht nix *besides nothing;* drvun *thereof;* eens *one;* zwoe *two;* keens *none;* unner *under;* druff *on;* johr *year;* wohr *true;* kummt rei [PG. rei] *come in;* no no; jetz' *now;* gedenkt *supposed;* fraa *woman;* kopp *head;* weesz *knows;* meeschter *master;* e' gut' *kind a good child.*

The South German dialect of Breisgau has G. *er hilft* (he helps, PG. ær helft), *g'seit* (as in Alsatia) for *gesagt,* PG. 'ksaat,' *us* for G. and PG. 'aus,' *i* for *ich, herrli* for *herrlich,* (PG. hærrlich), *wön* for *wollen, zit* (as in Alsatia) for *zeit, aue* for *augen* (eyes, PG. aughə, Alsat. auə), *de* for *du, gen* for *gegeben* (given, PG. gewwə, sometimes suppressing *ge-,* to which attention has been called). Besides *gen,* the following Allemanic example (Radlof, 2, 99) contains *wore* for *geworden,* and *uskratzt* for *ausgekratzt—*

"Se han kurzwilt un Narrethei triebe, un am End isch der Hirt keck wore, un het em Mümmele e Schmützle gen, un se het em seldrum d'Aue nit uskratzt."

They trifled and fooled, and finally the shepherd (ist keck geworden) *became bold, and* (hat gegeben) *gave* (dem) *to the water nymph a kiss, and she did not* (dasselbe darum) *on-that-account* ('em' for *ihm*) *scratch out his eyes.*

In the following examples, the Breisgauish and PG. are probably more nearly allied than might be supposed from a comparison of the spelling. The Alsatian and PG. are in the same alphabet.

German.	Breisgau.	Alsace.	PG.	English.
regenbogen,	regeboge,	râjəbâu-ə,	reeghəboogho,	*rainbow.*
wo, von,	wu, vun,	wuu, fun,	wuu, fun,	*where, of.*
da, mal,	do, mol,	doo, mool,	doo, mool,	*here, times.*
schaf,	schof,	schoof,	schoof,	*sheep.*
schlafen,	schlofe,	schloofə,	schloofə,	*to sleep.*
und, gelt,	un, gel,	un, gel,	un, gel,	*and, truly !*
wohnen,	wuhne,	woonə,	wuunə,	*to reside.*
kommen,	kumme,	kummə,	kummə,	*to come.*
gesehen,	g'sehne,	g'sên,	kseenə,	*seen.*
jahr, auch,	johr, au,	joor, au,	joor, aa,	*year, also.*
nachbar,	nochber,	nochbər,	nochbər,	*neighbor.*
nicht, nichts,	nit, nix,	net, niks,	net, niks,	*not, nothing.*
selbiger,	seller,	tsellər,	sellər,	*that one.*

German.	Breisgau.	Alsace.	PG.	English.
es ist jetzt,	's isch jetz,	əs isch jets,	s isch jets,	*it is now.*
etwas,	ebbes,	eppəs,	ebbəs, eppəs,	*something.*
nunmehr,	nummee,	(nimmə),	nummi,	*now.*
darunter,	runter,	(nuntər),	runtər,	*under.*
als, einem,	as, eme,	as, əmə,	as, mə,	*as, to a.*
man kann,	mer kann,	m'r kann,	mər kann,	*one can.*
sie haben,	sie hen, han,	sii haan,	sii hen,	*they have.*
wir sind,	mer sin,	m'r sin,	m'r sin,	*we are.*
weiszt,	wescht,	weischt,	weoscht,	*knowest.*
das, hat,	des, het,	des, hot,	des, hət,	*the, has.*

In the next three lines of Breisgauish (Radlof, 2, 95) words which agree more or less with PG. are in italic—

"*Do isch au kei Plätzle meh,*	Here is also no spot more,
Wu i könnt *mi* Haupt[1] *hinlege,*	where I might my head repose,
Wenn i *vun der Arbet geh.*"	when I from my work depart.

The following (Radlof, 2, 92) is also in the Breisgau dialect:

Siehsch de, Kind, de Regeboge, ...	Seest thou child the rainbow, ...
Gel, das isch e Pracht vun Farbe, ...	truly it is a glory of color, ...
Noeh het jetz mit de Sine	Noah has now with (the) his [people]
E Johannisfirle g'macht,	made a (midsummer) Johannes-fire[2]
Un in Herrlikeit un Pracht	and in splendor and glory
Isch der Herr debi erschine,	the Lord (dabei) thereat appeared,
Un zum Noeh het er g'sproche :	and to Noah has he spoken:
Guck, e Zeiche setz i fest,	Behold, a sign I firmly set [me,
Wil de Fride mit mer hest,	whilst thou (hast) keepst peace with
's Wort des hab i niemol broche	the word—that have I never broken
Un de Herr het's Wort au g'halte,	and the Lord has the word also kept,
Den der Regeboge steht,	for the rainbow stands
Wenn Gott au im Wetter geht,	whenever God goes in the tempest,
Un er loszt de Zorn nit walte.	and he (läszt) allows not (den) the [anger to rule.

[1] Scarcely PG., ' kəp ' (G. kopf) being used.
[2] See Pulleyn's Etym. Compendium, 1853, at BONE-FIRES. [See also, Jacob Grimm, *Deutsche Mythologie,* pp. 567-597, for fires generally, and pp. 583-593, for these Midsummer fires in particular.—*A. J. Ellis.*]

CHAPTER VIII.

EXAMPLES.

§ 1. *Wüdər aa‚geschmiirt.*

¶ 1. Dass dii meed ən wunnərbaarər schtəff sin, wen [wann?] sii f'r mennə ausgrukə, wærd iir aa schun ausgefunnə hawə. Sii sin so schlippərich wii ən fisch, un wan m'r meent m'r hätt eens fescht, dan knabbərt 's schun an nər annərə ang'l.

TRICKED AGAIN.—*That the maidens are a wondrous matter if they (ausgucken) look out for husbands (werdet Ihr) will you (auch) also have (schon) already discovered. They are as slippery as a fish, and when one supposes (subjunctive or hätte) he might-have one fast, (it nibbles) there is already nibbling at (einer andern) another hook.*

¶ 2. Ich hab eich do schun foor 'səm' tseit tsrik f'rtseelt, wii ich mit d'r 'Hœnnə' ei‚kummə bin, un was f'r 'kœlkəlcesch'nəs' dass ich gemacht hab f'r n 'schtoor' úftsusétsə an dem alti Schniipikl seinər kreits-schtross.

I have recounted (euch) to you here 'some' time ago, how I paid attentions to 'Hannah,' and the 'calculations' that I made to set up [an English idiom] a 'store' at old Schniepickel's Crossroads.

¶ 3. 'Well,' selli tseit hab ich mich bei d'r 'Hœnnə' wiischt aa‚geschmiirt gefunnə (kfunnə), f'r ich hab gemeent, dass sii niimand sunscht 'gleichə,' un liiwər drei moonat lang gebrootənə rattə fressə deet, wii an eenighər annərər kœrl tsu denkə—

'Well,' that time I found myself badly[1] tricked with 'Hannah,' for I believed that she 'liked' nobody else, and (thät liebor fressen) would rather devour fried rats three months long, than to think on any other fellow ;

¶ 4. un dii 'seem' tseit hat sii dem 'Sæm' Hinnərbee‚ 'kumpanii' gewwə, un tsu annəri ksaat, sii wott sich lüwər ufhenkə un

---

[1] A Swiss use of the G. wüst (waste, confused, wild).

4

d'r hals mit d'r həls-seeg apschneidə, as so ən alt 'griinharn' wii
mich heiərə.

*and the ' same' time she gave ' Sam' Hinterbein 'company,' and said
to others, she would rather hang herself and cut off the neck with the
wood-saw* (als) *than to marry such an old greenhorn as me.*

¶ 5. Du kannscht diir denkə, dass mich sel f'rtsernt hət un dass
ich mei, 'plæns' weeghə schtoorhaltə an dem kreitsweek pletslich
ge-ennərt hab.

You can imagine to yourself that that (verzürnt) *angered me, and
that* (plötzlich) *suddenly I* (habe geändert) *changed my plans about
storekeeping at the Crossway.*

¶ 6. Ich hab mich dann ən bissl rúmgegúkt un gefúnnə dass
drəwə an d'r 'Passəm krik' ən 'neisi opning' f'r n tíchtighər
'schmærtər' kærl wii ich eenər bin, wær.

I then looked me (ein biszchen herum) *a little round and* (gefunden)
found that (droben) *up on ' Possum creek' was a ' nice opening ' for a*
(tüchtig *tight) capable ' smart' fellow, as I am one.*

¶ 7. Dart am ek wuunt d'r alt 'Eeb' Windbeissər uf m groosi
schtik land ; dem sei, 'Meeri' hət m'r 'əbaut' aa,kschtannə, un
alləs sunscht dart rum hət m'r recht guut gefállə (kfallə), juscht
hət dii 'Meeri' so gaar eewich fiil schweschtər un briidər, dass als
kee, plats f'r uns tswee im haus waar, un in dii scheir geeə musstə,
wann m'r mit ən-annər schwetsə wəttə.

There on the corner lives old 'Abe' Windbeisser on a large piece (of)
land ; whose ' Mary about' pleased me, and all (sonst dort herum)
besides there-about pleased me right well, only Mary had (gar ewig so
viel) *quite ever so many sisters and brothers, that* (there) *was always
no place for us two in the house, and* (we) *must go in the barn when
we would speak with oneanother.*

¶ 8. Sell hət m'r 'əf-koors' net so árik aa,kschtannə, awər
(aawər) dii Meeri hət gemeent des wær niks, m'r misst sich ewwə
tsu helfə wissə.

*That 'of-course' was not so very agreeable to me, but Mary con-
sidered that to be nothing ; one must know* (eben) *exactly how to help
one's self.*

¶ 9. En tseit lang iss 'nau' alləs guut gangə, meini 'kælkə-
leeschənss' waarə wiidər 'reddi' un dii Meeri hət mir tsu
f'rschteeə gewwə, dass ich eenichə tseit mit iirəm daadi schwetsə
un dann d'r parrər [and parrə] beschtéllə kennt.

(*For*) *some time* '*now*' *all went well, my* '*calculations*' *were again* '*ready*,' *and Mary had given me to understand that any time I could speak with her* (Swiss dädi) *father, and then engage the minister.*

¶ 10. ' Well,' d'r neekscht sundaak, ich hab iim ksaat dass ich un sei‚ Meeri unsər meind ufgemacht hättə tsu heiərə, un froog iin ep œr eenich eppəs [or ebbəs] dageeghə hätt. Nee‚, secht œr, ich hab niks dageeghə, aawər hoscht du dann dii ' Mœndə ' heit kseene?

' *Well*' *the next Sunday I told him that I and his Mary had* (English idiom) *made up our* '*mind*' *to marry, and asked him* (ob) *if he had* (einiges etwas) *any* (some)*thing there-against. No,* (*sagt*, for G. sagte) *said he, I have nothing against it—but have you seen* '*Amanda*' *today?*

¶ 11. "Iir hen mich lets f'rschtannə," saag ich, "ich will dii Meeri heiərə, net dii Mœndə." (Du muscht wissə, dii Mœndə iss 'əbaut' seks joor eltər wii dii Meeri un net neekscht soo guutgukich.)

" *You have understood me* [Swiss and SG. letz] *wrongly,*" *say I,* "*I wish to marry* ' *Mary* ' *and not* ' *Amanda*'." (*You must know,* '*Amanda* ' *is* ' *about* ' *six years older than* ' *Mary*,' *and not* (next) *near so goodlooking.*)

¶ 12. "Joo, ich hab dich recht guut f'rschtanuə, aawər du bischt noch net ' ufgepooscht.' Geschtər marighə iss dii Mœndə nooch ' Hen' Greifdaalərs ' schtoor ' un hət sich eppəs kaaft—' Griischən ' Bendər glaab ich heescht sii des ding.

" *Yes, I have understood you right well, but you are not yet* '*posted*' *up. Yesterday morning* '*Amanda*' *went to* ' *Hen.* ' *Gripedollar's* ' *store* ' *and bought herself something—* ' *Grecian* ' *Bend* (pun on *bend* and *bänder*, ribbons,) *I believe she calls the thing.*

¶ 13. " Wii dii Meeri sel geseenə (or kseenə) hət, wœrd sii gans (or gants) närrisch dofoor', un fangt aa‚ mit d'r Mœndə tsu handlə, weil d'r ' schtoorkiipər ' juscht dii eéntsighə maschiin katt hət.

When Mary saw it she becomes quite silly (dafür) *for it, and begins to bargain with Amanda, as the* ' *storekeeper*' (hat gehabt) *had but the single machine.*

¶ 14. " Well, sii sin net eenich [geworden] warrə bis geeghə oowət, un dann hen sii 'əgriid,' das dii Meeri dich tsu d'r Mœndə ufgept, un dii Mceri dii Griischən Bendər kriikt !'"

" *Well, they were not* (einig) *in accord till* (gegen abend) *towards evening, and then they ' agreed' that Mary would give you up to Amanda, and she should get the Grecian Bend.*"

¶ 15. F'*rschwappt?* Mich uf den 'Griischən' Bendər 'f'rschwappt,' oone mich ærscht tsu frooghə?!

'*Swapped*'*! Me* '*swapped*' *on the Grecian Bend,* (ohne mich erst zu fragen) *without first asking me?!*

¶ 16. "So schteet s 'nau,' dii Mændə is drunnə im kuuschtall, wann du fileicht ærscht mit iir dərweeghə schwetsə witt."

"*So stands it* '*now,*' *Amanda is* (darunter) *down there at. the stable, if you perhaps* (willst) *will first speak with her about it.*"

¶ 17. Ich? mit iir dərweeghə schwetsə? Iss gaar net nootwennich! Wann mich deini meed kaafə, f'rkaafə un f'*rschwappə* kennə, dann sollə sii aa seenə, dass sii mich kriighə. 'Guutbei.'

I? speak with her about it? (*It*) *is quite unnecessary. If your girls* (können kaufen) *can buy, sell, and ' swap' me, then* (sollen sie auch sehen) *shall they also see that they get me.* ' *Goodby.*'

¶ 18. Ich wees net was dii Windbeissər meed[1] mit un oone Griischən Bendər fun miir denkə, aawər was ich fun iinə denk wees ich, wærd diir s aawər 'ennihau' net saaghə.

I know not what the Windbeisser girls with and without Grecian Bend think of me, (aber ich weiss) *but I know what I think of them— but will ' anyhow' not tell it to you.*

¶ 19. 'Nau' hab ich im sinn noch eé₁mool[2] tsu prowiirə, sobál ich n 'tschænss' ausfinn, un wann m'r s aa dann net glikt, geb ich s uf un wærd ən altər 'bætschələr.'[3]

I now have in mind (zu probîren) *to try yet* (einmal) *once, as soon as I find out a ' chance,' and if it also prospers not then with me, I will give it up and be an old ' bachelor.'*

§ 2.   *Wii kummt əs?*

¶ 1. Ich lees eiər tseitung 'reglər' alli woch, un weil ich alsfnrt so fiil nei-ichkeit'n drin lees, do bin ich schun oft (əft) uf dii 'nosch'n' [gekommen] kummə iir [müsset] misst alləs wissə.

[1] This 'meed' is singular and plural, but the singular is more commonly meedl, SG. maidle, G. mädchen. It differs from maad (sing. and pl. G. *magd*), a female servant.
[2] Being emphasised, the accent is on the first syllable, while in ' əmool' (below § 2, ¶ 3) it is on the second.
[3] Condensed and transliterated from the (German) *Bucks Caunty Express*, Doylestown, Pa. July 20, 1869.

How comes it? *I read* (euer) *your journal 'regular' every week, and as I constantly read so many novelties in it,* (da *then*) *have I indeed often come to the 'notion' you must know everything.*

¶ 2. Wann epper sich ufhengt, ədər heiərt, ədər eppəs schteelt, ədər gœrn ən guuti 'affis' hätt, ədər in dii 'tscheel' kummt, ədər sich n fing-er apschneidt, ədər sei, 'plats' f'rkaaft, ədər n hinkl schteelt, ədər 'guuf'rniir'' wærrə will, ədər im 'gəttər' kfunnə wært, ədər seini tscitung net betsaalt, danu kann m'r sich druf f'rlassən, dass əs in dii tseitung kummt.

If (Swiss *epper,* masc. of G. etwas,) *anyone hangs himself, or marries, or steals* (G. etwas) *anything, or would like to have a good 'office,' or gets into 'jail,' or cuts himself a finger off, or sells his 'place'* (or *farm*), *or steals a chicken, or wishes to become 'governor,' or is* [gefunden] *found in the 'gutter,' or does not pay for his journal, then one can depend upon it that it gets into the newspaper.*

¶ 3. Ich bin ən altər bauər un f'rschtee net fiil, un weil iir alles tsu wissə scheint, doo will ich eich əmoól ən paar sachə frooghə, dii ich gœrn wissə deet.

I am an old farmer and do not understand much, and as you seem to understand everything, I will here ask you once several things, which I would like to know.

¶ 4. Wii kummt əs, dass dii jung-i bauərəbuuwə graad brillən un schtək traaghə missə, wann sii in dii 'kallitsch' [geschickt werden] kschikt wœrrə? Ich hab als gemeent ich wollt mei, 'Sœm' aa in dii 'kallitsch' schikə, aawər wann dii leit graad schlechti aaghə kriighə un laam wœrrə, dann behalt ich mei, 'Sœm' liiwər dəheem un lœrn iin selwər als oowəts.

How comes it, that the young farmer-boys must immediately carry spectacles and (stöcke) *sticks when they are sent to 'college'? I have hitherto thought I would send my 'Sam.' to 'college,' but if people immediately get bad eyes and become lame, I will rather keep him at home and teach him myself of evenings.*

¶ 5. Wii kummt əs, dass deel weipsleit in eirəm .iistən (Easton) soo aarm [sein wollen] sei, wellə un doch soo lang-i frackschwents uf 'm 'peefmənt' noochschleefə? [Werden] wœrre[1] selli weipsleit betsaalt f'r s 'peefmənt' [sauber] sauwər tsu haltə, ədər wii [können] kennə sii 'affoordə' soo aa, tsugeeə?

How comes it, that (theil) *part (of the) women in your Easton* (sein wollen) *pretend to be so poor, and yet* (nach-schleifen) *drag along*

---

[1] G. *worden* becomes 'warrə.' See § 1, ¶ 14.

such long frock (schwänze) tails on the 'pavement'? Will those women be paid for keeping the 'pavement' clean, else how can they 'afford' to proceed thus?

¶ 6. Wii kummt əs, dass dii jung-i buuwə selli meed, woo reichi, daadis [Swiss dädi] hen, liiwər noochschpringə als dii aarmi? Gukt sel net als wii wann sii meer uum s geld gewwə [thäten] dcetə als wii uum dii meed? Wann ich ən meedl wœr un hätt so ən 'boo,' dann deet ich iin mit d'r fciərtsang fartschtéwərə.

How comes it, that the young men (lieber nachspringen) sooner run after those girls who have rich [the plural -s is English] fathers, than the poor ones? Looks it not just as if they would give more for the money than for the maid? If I were a girl and had such a 'beau,' (then) I would [stöbern, ö long] drive him forth with the fire-tongs.

¶ 7. Wii kummt əs, dass n deel jung-i leit nimmi dcitsch leesə un schwetsə kennə, wann sii mool 'jes' un 'noo' saaghə kennə? Meim [dative for genitive] nochbər, dem Maardi Halsbendl sei, cltəst'r [sohn] suu, dær so deitsch waar wii saurkraut dcs schun siwwə mool ufgwærmt iss, waar kærtslich əmool in d'r schtatt, un wii ær wiid'r heem kummə iss, do waar ær so eng-lisch, dass ær schiir gaar nimmi mit seim daadi un mammi schwctsə kann. Sii sin 'nau' arik im 'truwl' un sei, daadi meent, sii misst'n iin naus nooch Kniphaus'n schikkə, f'r iin wiid'r (widr) deitsch tsu machə.

How comes it that some young people are no longer able to read and speak German if they only know how to say 'yes' and 'no'? The eldest son of my neighbor Martin Neckband, who was as Dutch as sourcrout which has been warmed up seven times, was once recently a week in town, and when he had returned home again, there was he so English that he could scarcely speak anymore with his father and mother. They are 'now' greatly in 'trouble,' and his father thinks they must send him out to Kniphausen to make him German again.

¶ 8. Wie kummt əs, dass dii aarmi leit geweenlich dii meerschtən hund un katsə hen? Do bei uns wuunt n famíljə, dii als bettələ muss, un dii fiir groosə hund un siwwə katsə hət. Sii selwər saaghə, sii misst'n so fiil hund hawə f'r dii diib aptsuhaltə.[1]

How comes it, that poor people (gewöhnlich haben) commonly have the most dogs and cats? Here near us lives a family which must always beg, and which has four large dogs and seven cats. They themselves say, they (müszten haben) were obliged to have so many dogs to keep away the thieves.

[1] Condensed from the (German) *Correspondent & Demokrat*, Easton, Pa. Aug. 25, 1869.

§ 3.

<table>
<tr><td>

Will widd'r Biiwəli[1] *sei,.*

¶ 1.

.əs reeghərt heit, mr kann net naus
un ə iss so 'loonsəm' doo im haus;
  mr wees net wii mr fiilt.
ich will mool duu, als wœœr ich klee,
un uf d'r éwərscht schpeichər gee,
  dart hab ich uftmools kschpiilt.

¶ 2.

.ən biiwli bin ich widdər jets,
wu sin mei, k r u t s ə un mei, klets?
  nau wœrt n haus gebaut!
əs schpiilt sich doch net guut alée,—
ich bin joo doch kee, biiwli mee!
  was kluppt mei, hœrts so laut!

¶ 3.

Harrich! was 'n wunnərbaarə sach!
d'r reeghə rapplt uf 'm dach
  gaar nimmi wii ær hət!
ich hab 's als kœært mit leichtəm bærts,
nau gepts m'r arik heemwee schmœrts,
  kennt heilə wan ich wət.

¶ 5.

Des schpiilə geet net, səl ich fart?
was iss uf selli balkə dart?
  'nau' bin ich widdər buu!
dart hen m'r keschtə ausgeschtreit,
tsu dœrrə uf dii Krischdaak tseit—
  deet 's gleichə widdər duu!

¶ 6.

.ən biiwli sei,—sell iss d'r wært—
dii keschtə 'rooschtə' uf d'r hært—
  was hət des als gekracht!
Sell iss forbei. Ich fiil 's im gmiid,[2]
es schpiilt 'n rechtəs heemwee liid,
  d'r reeghə uf 'm dach!

¶ 7.

Dort schteet dii 'seem' alt walnus kischt,
ich wunnər 'nau' was dart drin isch?
  's muss eppəs 'bartich sei,.
Kallénər, tseitung, bichər—hoo!
dii alti sachə hen sii doo
  all sunnərscht-sewərscht[3] nei,.

</td><td>

Will be a Boy again.

1.

It rains to-day, one cannot out,
and t is so 'lonesome' in the house;
  one knows not how one feels,
I will once do as were I small
and in the highest garret go—
  there have I ofttimes played.

2.

An urchin am I now again,
where are my corn-cobs and my blocks?
  'now' will a house be built!
one plays indeed not well alone—
I am in fact no urchin more!
  my heart how loud it beats!

3.

And hark! how wonderful it is!
the rain now rattles on the roof
  no more as it once did!
I heard it once with buoyant heart,
but now it gives a home-sick smart,
  I could weep if I would.

5.

The play succeeds not, shall I forth?
what is upon that timber there?
  'now' I 'm a boy again!
there did we spread the chesnuts out
to have them dry for Christmas time—
  would 'like' to do t again!

6.

To be a boy—that is worth while—
to 'roast' the chesnuts on the harth—
  what crackling that produced!
t is gone—I feel that in my soul
it plays a real home-sick tune—
  the rain upon the roof!

7.

There stands the 'same' old walnut chist,
I wonder 'now' what may be in t,
  it must be something (abartig) rare.
Books—calendars—newspapers—oh
the olden objects have we here
  all upside down within.

</td></tr>
</table>

[1] The spelling of the original is 'Buwelle,' without the *umlaut*, which others use. The original has 'owerscht' in the fifth line, but the *umlaut* is in use, and seems to be required, as in Bavarian. For notes [2] and [3] see next page.

¶ 8.

'Nau' bin ich aawər recht ən buu,
weil ich do widdər seenə duu
des alt bekanntə sach.
Harrich! hæærscht d'r reeghə! 'Jes
indiid'—
er schpiilt ən rechtəs heemwee liid
dart oowə uf 'm dach!

¶ 13.

Sii henkə net am balkə mee
dii bindlə fun dem kreitər tee,
un allərlee gewærts;
'nau' will ich widdər biiwli sei,—
ich hool sii f'r dii mammi rei,—
sell 'pliist' mei, büwli hærts.[4]
— HARBAUGH.

8.

But 'now' I truly am a boy
because I now again behold
this old familiar thing.
Hark! Hearst the rain! 'Yes, yes
indeed,'
it plays a proper home-sick air
up there upon the roof!

13.

They hang not on the cross-beams more
the bundles of botanic tea,
and every kind of root;
'now' I will be a boy again
and for my mother bring them in—
that 'pleased' my boyish heart.

[2] G. gemüth.
[3] G. das *unterste* zu *oberst* (topsy-turvy).   Compare PG. 'hinnərscht-feddərscht'
(wrong end foremost).
[4] Transliterated extract from a longer poem in the *Father Abraham*, Lancaster,
Pa. Feb. 1869.

§ 4.   *Anglicised German.*

The following factitious example, full of English words and
idioms, is from a New York German newspaper, and purports
to be written by a German resident in America. The spelling
recalls the name HEYFLEYER over a stall in the stables of the
King of Wurtemberg. The writer of the letter spells his
name in three ways, instead of 'Schweineberger,' as given in
the tale.

Landkäsder, Penſilvenia, North-Amerika, 32. Dezr. 52.

Dheire Mudder!—Du Würſt es nit begreiſe kenne, alſz ich dort weck bin, ich
hawen alle Leit geſacht, der Hannes werrd nit gud ausmache, das ich jetzt ſo gut
ab binn. Awer, well, jetzt g'hör' ich zu de Tſchentel-Leit in unſre Zitti unn
eeniger Männ, wo in Iurop en werri fein Männ is, dhät lachche, bikahs er
gleichte ſo gut auszumache, als der John Swinebarker.

Obſchon, ich unterſtche des Büſſeneſſ beſſer as die andre Dotſchmänn, wo
eweri Teim ſo ſchlecht edſchukädet bleibe, as ſe in Iurop ware ; Wer hier gleicht,
gud auszumache, muſz ſich zu de amerikaniſche Tſchentel-Leit halte, wo eweri
Männ Something lerne kann.

Du kannſt auch zu mein dheires Eliänorche ſage, das es kommen kann ; ſie
kann der hohl Däy im Rockel-Schär ſitze, ich ſend hir inkluded ſixtig Dollars,
mit das kann ſie über Liwerpuhl und Nujork zu mich komme, und verbleibe
Dein moſt zänkvoll Son   John Swineberger.

Boſchkrippt: Du muſt die Monni for des Bordo auslege ; ich will ſend es Dir
mit dem nächſte Letter.   John Schweinebärker.

CHAPTER IX.

ENGLISH INFLUENCED BY GERMAN.

§ 1. *German Words introduced.*

If the Germans of Pennsylvania adopted many words from English, the English speaking population applied the appellation of *German* or *Dutch* to unfamiliar varieties of objects, such as a *Dutch cheese*, a *German lock;* or they adopted the original names, as in calling a form of curds *smearcase* (G. schmierkäse) in the markets and prices current. German forms of food have furnished the vicinal English with *sourcrout, mush, shtreisslers, bretsels, fawstnachts*,[1] *tseegercase, knep* (G. Knöpfe, the *k* usually pronounced), *bower-knep, noodles;* and in some of the interior markets, endive must be asked for under the name of ' œntiifi,' even when speaking English. Dutch gives *crullers*, but *stoop* (of a house) is hardly known. In English conversation one may hear expressions like " He belongs to the *freindschaft* " (he is a kinsman or relation); " It makes me *greisslich* to see an animal killed " (makes me shudder and revolt with disgust—turns my stomach). A strong word without an English equivalent.

The German idiom of using *einmal* (once) as an expletive, is common, as in "Bring me a chair once," and when a person whose vernacular is English says, " I am through another " (I am confused), he is using a translation of the German *durch einander*, PG. 'dárich onánner.' Of such introduced words, the following deserve mention.

Metsel-soup, originally pudding broth, the butcher's perquisite, but subsequently applied to a gratuity from the animals he has slaughtered.

[1] Shrove-tide cakes—with the PG. pronunciation, except *st.*

Shinner, G. schinder (a knacker,[1]) an objurgatory epithet applied by butchers to farmers who compete with them in the market.

Speck, the flitch of salt bacon, particularly when boiled with sour-crout, hence, 'speck and sourcrout.'

Tsitterly, calf's-foot jelly.

Hartley, a hurd-le for drying fruit.

Snits, a **snit** (G. schnitz, a cut), a longitudinal section of fruit, particularly apples, and when dried for the kitchen. The term is in use in districts where German is unknown.[2]

Hootsle, PG. hutsl, G. hotzel, a dried fruit; Bavar. and Suab. hutzel, a dried pear. In Pennsylvania, a peach dried without removing the stone.

Dumb (G. dumm) is much used for *stupid*.

Fockle (G. fackel), a fisherman's torch.

Mother (PG. from G. mutter-weh, not parturition, but) a hysterical rising in the throat. The word occurs in old and provincial English.[3]

Chipmunk, a ground-squirrel (Tamias); *chip* probably from its cry, and Swiss *munk*, a marmot.

Spook (G. Spuk), a spectre; and the verb, as—"It spooks there," "The grave-yard spooks."

Cristkintly (PG. Krischtkintli, G. Chrïst Kindlein), the Christ Child who is supposed to load the chrïstmas trees and bring presents at christmas. Perverted in the Philadelphia newspapers to *Kriss Kringle*, *Kriss Kingle*, and *Kriss Kinkle*.

Christmas-tree, a well-known word for a well-known and much used object, but absent from the American dictionaries.

Bellsnickle, PG. beltsnikkl (G. *Pelz* a pelt, skin with hair, as a bear-skin, here used as a disguise, and perhaps associated with *peltzen,* to pelt,) and *Nickel, Nix,* in the sense of a demon. (Suab. Pelzmärte, as if based on *Martin*). A masked and hideously disguised person, who goes from house to house on christmas eve, beating (or pretending to beat) the children and servants, and throwing down nuts and cakes before leaving. A noisy party

---

[1] G. Knochen (bones).

[2] A teacher asked a class—If I were to cut an apple in two, what would you call one of the pieces? "A *half.*" And in four? "A *fourth.*" And if I cut it in eight equal pieces, what would one of them be? "A *snit!*"

[3] Compare—O, how this mother swells up toward my heart!
      Hysterica passio, thou climbing sorrow,
      Thy element's below.—*King Lear*, act 2, sc. 4, speech 20, v. 54.
                        —*A. J. Ellis.*

accompanies him, often with a *bell*, which has influenced the English name.

These, I suppose, were Christmas mummers, though I heard them called "Bell-schnickel."—*Atlantic Monthly*, October, 1869, p. 484.

Gounsh, n. and v.i. As *to seesaw* implies reciprocal motion, so *to gounsh* is to move up and down, as upon the free end of an elastic board. PG. 'Kumm, mr wello gaunscho.' (Come, let us gounsh.) Suab. gautschen; Eng. to *jounce*.[1]

Hoopsisaw (PG. húppsisaa, also provincial German). A rustic or low dance, and a lively tune adapted to it. Inferior lively music is sometimes called 'hoopsisaw music,' 'a hoopsisaw tune.'[2]

Hoove, v.i. a command to a horse to back, and used by extension as in "The men hooved (demurred) when required to do more work." Used in both senses in the Swiss *hüfen*, imperative *hüf!* and Schmeller (*Bayr. Wörterb*. 2, 160) gives it as Bavarian.

Hussling-, or **Hustling-match**, PG. hossl-mætsch (with English *match*), a raffle. From the root of *hustle*, the game being conducted by shaking coins in a hat and counting the resulting heads.

Sock up, "to make a man sock up," pay a debt, produce his *sack* or pouch. This is uncertain, because, were a PG. expression to occur like "Du muscht ufsakko " (you must sock up), it might be borrowed from English.

Boof, peach brandy. In Westerwaldish, *buff* is water-cider,—cider made by wetting the pomace and pressing it a second time.

Sots, n. sing. G. satz, home-made 'yeast' as distinguished from 'brewer's-east.'

Sandman, "The sandman is coming,"—said when children get sleepy about bedtime and indicate it by rubbing the eyes. Used thus in Westerwald and Suabia.[3] Children are warned against touching dirt by the exclamation (bæætschi).

Snoot, for snout, a widespread teutonic form.

---

[1] The German word appears to be *gautschen* without the *n*. So Schmeller (Bayerisches Wörterbuch, 2, 87) "*gautschen, getschen*, schwanken, schaukeln." Adelung (Wörterbuch der hochdeutschen Mundart, 2, 439) explains it as a technical paper-maker's word for taking the sheets out of the mould and laying them upon the press-board, *Gautschbret*. He adds that a carrying chair was formerly called a *Gautsche*, and refers it to *Kutsche* and French *coucher*.—*A. J. E.*

[2] Compare Papageno's song in Mozart's *Zauberflöte* :
Der Vogelfänger bin ich ja
Stets lustig, heisa, hopsasa.—*A. J. Ellis.*

[3] Known probably throughout England. Known to me, a Londoner, from earliest childhood.—*A. J. Ellis.*

§ 2. *Family Names Modified.*

With several concurrent languages, the deterioration of names is an obvious process. Among the mixed population of Baltimore, the name 'Bradley' is to a Frenchman *Bras-de-long;* for 'Strawberry' (alley) and 'Havre-de-grâce' (in Maryland) the Germans say *Strubbel*, and *Hasel-im-gras;* and the Irish make the following changes—

Carron (French)	*Scarron*	Schöffeler	*Scofield*
Coquerelle	*Corcoran*	van Dendriessche	*Driscol*
de Vries	*Freezer*	van Emstede	*Hampsted*
Giessen	*Gleason*	Winsiersski	*Winchester*
Grimm	*Grimes*	Fayette Street	*Faith St.*
Henning	*Hannon*	Alice Ann St.	*Alexander St.*
Rosier	*Rosetree*	Happy Alley	*Apple Alley*

A German with a name which could not be appreciated, was called *John Waterhouse* because he attended a railroad tank—a name which he adopted and placed upon his sign when he subsequently opened a small shop. A German family became ostensibly Irish by preferring the sonant phase of their initial —calling and writing themselves *Grady* instead of Krady; a name 'Leuter' became *Lander;* 'Amweg' was tried a while as *Amwake* and then resumed; and in a family record, the name 'George' is given as *Schorts.* A postoffice 'Chickis' (Chikiswalungo—place where crayfish burrow) received a letter directed to *Schickgets,* another *Schickens Laenghaéster Caunte,* and 'Berks County' has been spelled *Burgix Caunte.*[1]

The following German and Anglicised forms may be compared,—

Albrecht	*Albright*	Frey (free)	*Fry*
Bachman	*Baughman*	Früauf	*Freeauf*
Becker	*Baker, Pecker*	Fusz (foot)	*Foose*
Dock	*Duck*	Geisz (goat)	*Gise*
Eberhardt	*Everhart*	Gerber	*Garber*
Eberle	*Everly*	Giebel	*Gibble*
Eckel	*Eagle*	Gräff	*Graff*, -o, -ae
Ege[2]	*Hagy ?*	Guth	*Good, Goot*
Ewald	*Evalt*	Haldeman	*Holderman*[3]
Fehr	*Fair*	Herberger	*Harberger*

[1] The geographical names at the close of Chapter I. p. 6, are Kentucky, Safe Harbor, Syracuse, and Pinegrove. The drugs are aloes (pronounced as in Latin!), paregoric, citrine ointment, acetic acid, hiera picra, cinnamon, Guiana pepper, gentian, cinchona, opium, hive syrup, senna and manna mixed, sulphate of zink, corrosive sublimate, red precipitate, aniline, logwood, Epsom salts, magnesia, cordial, cubebs, bichromate of potash, valerian (G. Báldrian), laurel berries, cochineal.   [2] Rhymes plaguey, even in English localities.

[3] As if from the plant *elder,* instead of Swiss halde, a *steep* or *declivity*—the name being Swiss.

Hinkel	*Hinkle*	Pfautz	*Fouts, Pouts*
Hofman	*Hoofman*	Pfeiffer	*Pyfer*
Huber	*Hoover*	Reif (ripe)	*Rife*
Kaufman	*Coffman*	Reisinger	*Riesinger*
Kaufroth	*Cuffroot*	Riehm	*Ream*
Kohler	*Kaylor*	Roth (red)	*Roath, Rote*
Kochenauer	*Goughnour*	Ruth	*Root*
Koick	*Cowhawk*	Schellenberger	*Shallyberger* [1]
Krauskopf	*Krosskop*	Schenk	*Shank*
Kreider	*Crider*	Scheuerman	*Shireman*
Kreybil	*Graypeel*	Schnebele	*Snavely*
Kühnlein	*Coonly, -ley*	Schneider	*Snyder, Snider*
Kutz	*Kutts*	Seip	*Sype, Sipe*
Leitner	*Lightner*	Seipel	*Seiple, Sible*
Leybach	*Libough*	Seitz	*Sides*
Mayer	*Moyer*	Senz	*Sense*
Meyer	*Mire*	Spraul	*Sprowl*
Mosser	*Musser*	Stambach	*Stambough*
Mosseman	*Musselman*	Strein	*Strine*
Neumeyer	*Narmire?*	Valentin	*Felty*
Noll	*Null*	WeltzhuBer	*Beltzhoo Ver* [2]
Nüssli	*Nicely, Nissly*	Wetter	*Fetter*
Oberholtzer	*Overholser*	Wild	*Wilt*

So 'Schleyermacher' passed thro *Slaremaker* to *Slaymaker*; and by a similar process, farther changes may take place, like Mutsch to *Much*, Bertsch to *Birch*, Brein to *Brine*, Schutt to *Shoot* or *Shut*, Rüppel to *Ripple*, Knade (gnade *grace*) to *Noddy* Buch to *Book*, Stahr to *Star*, Fing-er to *Fin-ger*, Melling-er to *Mellin-jer*, Stilling-er[3] to *Stillin-jer*, Cover to *Cover*, Fuhrman to *Foreman*, Rohring[4] to *Roaring*, Gehman to *Gayman*.

Names are sometimes translated, as in *Stoneroad* for 'Steinweg,' *Carpenter* for both 'Schreiner' and 'Zimmermann,' and both *Short* and *Little* for 'Kurz' or 'Curtius.'

Part of a name may be anglicised, as in Fink*bine*, Espen*shade*, Traut*wine*—where the first syllable has the German sound. Fentz*maker* is probably a condensation of Fenstermacher.

It is remarkable that speakers of German often use English forms of baptismal names, as *Mary* for María, *Henry* for

---

[1] And Shellabarger, American Minister to Portugal, 1869.
[2] The 'b' and 'v' of the two forms have changed place.
[3] These names, with Rauch, Bucher, the Scotch Cochran, etc., are still pronounced correctly in English speaking localities in Pennsylvania; and at Harrisburg, 'Salade' rhymes *holid'y*.
[4] The organists Thunder and Rohr gave a concert in Philadelphia some years ago. In New York I have seen the names 'Stone and Flint,' and 'Lay and Hatch,' where the proper name takes précedence.

Heinrich, and *John* (tschan, shorter than the medial English sound) for Johannes.[1]

Of curious family names without regard to language, the following may be recorded—premising that proper names are especially subject to be made spurious by the accidents of typography.[2]

Ahl, Awl, Ammon, Annĕ, Barndollar, Baud, Bezoar, Bigging, Blades, Bohrer, Boring, Book, Bracken, Bricker (bridger), Buckwalter, Burkholder and Burch-halter (burg-holder), Byler, Candle, Candour, Care, Case, Channell, Chronister, Condit, Cooher, Cumberbus (Smith's Voyage to Guinea, 1744), Curgus or Circus, Dehoof, Dialogue, Ditto, Dosh, Eave, Eldridge (in part for Hildreth), Erb, Eyde, Eyesore (at Lancaster, Pa.), Fassnacht (G. fastnacht *shrovetide*), Feather, Ferry (for the Walloon name Ferree[3]); Friday, Fornaux, Furnace, Gans (*goose*, Gansert, Gensemer, Grossgensly), Gift (poison), Ginder, Gruel, Gutmann (good--man) Hag (hedge), Harmany, Hecter, Hepting, Herd, Heard, Hergelrat (rath *counsel*), Hinderer, Hock, Holzhauer and Holzhower (woodchopper), Honnafusz (G. hahn *a cock*), Kash, Kitch, Koffer, Landtart, Lawer, Leis, Letz, Licht, Line, Lipp, Lœb (lion), Lœwr (at St. Louis), Mackrel, Manusmith, Matt, Marrs, Mehl, Mortersteel, Mowrer (G. maur *a wall*), Napp, Neeper (Niebuhr?), Nohaker, Nophsker, Ochs, Over, Oxworth, Peelman, Penas (in Ohio), Pfund, Popp, Pontch, Quirk, Rathvon (Rodfong, Rautfaung), Road, Rottenstein (in Texas), Rutt, Sangmeister, Scheuerbrand, Schlegelmilch, Schlong (snake), Schœttel, Segar, Seldomridge, Senn, Service (in Indiana), Shaver, Shilling, Shinover, Shock, Shot, Showers, Skats (in Connecticut), Smout, Spoon, Springer, Steer (in Texas), Stern, Stetler, Stormfeltz, Strayer, Stretch, Stridle, Sumption, Surgeon, Swoop (a Suab-ian), Test, Tise, Tice (Theiss?), Tittles, Towstenberier, Tyzat (at St. Louis), Umble, Venus, Venerich, -rik, Vestal (in Texas), Vinegar('s Ferry, on the Susquehanna), Vogelsang, Wallower, Waltz, Wolfspanier, Wonder, Wool-rick (for Wulfrich?), Work, Worst, Yaffe, Yecker, Yeisley, Yordea, Zeh, Zugschwerdt.

---

[1] In the following inscription on a building, 'bei' instead of 'von' shows an English influence. The author knew English well: was a member of the state legislature, had a good collection of English—but not of German books—and yet preferred a German inscription—

ERBAUET BEI JOHN & MARIA HALDEMAN 1790.

Inscriptions are commonly in the roman character, from the difficulty of cutting the others.

[2] As in 'Chladori' for *Chladni*, in the American edition of the Westminster Review for July, 1865. The name Slyvons stands on the title-page as the author of a book on Chess (Bruxelles, 1856), which M. Cretaine in a similar work (Paris, 1865) gives as Solvyns. Upon calling Mr. C.'s attention to this point, he produced a letter from the former, signed *Solvyns*.

[3] The forms of this name are Ferree, Ferrie, Fuehre, Ferie, Verre, Fiere, Firre, Ferry, Feire, Fire; and as 'Ferree' is now pronounced *Free*, this may be a form also. In the year 1861, when in Nassau, I observed that the English visitors pronounced the name of a building in four modes, one German and three not German—Bâdhaus, Bath-house, Bad-house, and Bawd-house.

Among the following curious, incompatible, or hĭbrid[1]
names, titles (except that of 'General') have been mistaken
for proper names—Horatio Himmereich, Owen Reich, Caspar
Reed, Dennis Loucks, Baltzer Stone, Addison Shelp, Paris
Rudisill, Adam Schuh, Erasmus Buckenmeyer, Peter Pence,
General Wellington H. Ent, General Don Carlos Buel, Don
Alonzo Cushman, Sir Frank Howard, Always Wise (probably
for Alŏîs Weiss).   In November, 1867, Gilbert Monsieur
Marquis de Lafayette Sproul, asked the legislature of Tennes-
see to cut off all his names but the last two.

[1] Latin HIBRIDA.   I have marked the first English syllable short to dissociate
it from the *high-breed* of gardeners and florists, which 'hÿbrid' suggests.

CHAPTER X.

Imperfect English.

§ 1. *Broken English.*

Specimens of English as badly spoken by Germans who have an imperfect knowledge of it, are common enough, but they seldom give a proper idea of its nature. The uncertainty between sonant and surd is well known, but like the Cockney with *h*, it is a common mistake to suppose that the misapplication is universal,[1] for were this the case, the simple rule of reversal would set the speakers right in each case.

It is true that the German confounds English *t* and *d*, but he puts *t* for *d* more frequently than *d* for *t*. In an advertisement cut from a newspaper at Schwalbach, Nassau, in 1862—

Ordres for complet Diners or simples portions is punctually attented to and send in town—

there seems to be a spoken reversal of *t* and *d*, but I take 'send' to be an error of grammar, the pronunciation of the speaker being probably *attentet*, and *sent*. "Excuse my bad riding" (writing) is a perversion in speech. A German writes 'dacke' *take*, 'de' *the*, 'be' *be*, 'deere' *deer*, 'contra' *country*, and says :—

I am œbple [able] to accommodeted with any quantity of dis kins of Ruts [kinds of roots]. Plies tirectad to . . . Sout Frond Stread . . . nort america.

Here there is an attempt at the German flat *p* (p. 11) in the *bp* of 'able'; the surd *th* of 'north' and 'south' becomes *t*, and the sonant *th* of 'this' becomes *d*—'with' remaining under the old spelling. The *p* of 'please' remains, but *d* of 'direct' becomes *t*; and while final *t* of 'front' and 'street' becomes

---

[1] A boy in the street in Liverpool (1866) said to a companion—"'c told me to 'old up my 'ands an' I 'eld em up." He did not say *h*up, *h*an *h*I, *h*em.

d, the first *t* in 'street,' and that in 'directed,' are kept pure by surd *s* and *cay*. The rule of surd to surd and sonant to sonant is neglected in most of the factitious specimens of broken English.

The next is an instructive and a genuine example, being the record of a Justice of the Peace in Dauphin County (that of Harrisburg, the State Capital). It will be observed that the complainant bought a house, and being refused possession, makes a forcible entry and is resisted. The spelling is irregular, as in 'come' and 'com,' 'the' and 'de,' 'did' and 'dit,' 'then' and 'den,' 'nothin' and 'nosing,' 'house' and 'hause,' 'put' and 'but,' 'open' and 'upen.'

The said . . . sait I dit By de hause and I went in de hause at de back winder and den I dit upen de house and Dit take out his forniture and nobotty Dit disstorbe me till I hat his forniture out; I did but it out in de streat Before the house; and then he dit Com Wis a barl and dit nock at the dore that the Dore dit fly open and the molding dit Brack louse [1] and then I dit Wornt him not to come in the hause and not to put anneysing in the hause and he dit put in a barl Into the hause and I did put it out and he dit put it in again and then he did put In two Sisses [2] and srout the barl against Me; and then I dit nothin out annezmore and further nosing more; Sworn & Subscript the Dey and yeare above ritten before me . . . . J.P.—*Newspaper*.

The beginning and close follow a legal formula. The PG. idiom which drops the imperfect tense runs through this, in expressions such as 'I did open,' 'I did put,' 'I did warned,' etc.; but as might be expected, the English idiom is also present, in 'I went' and 'he throwed.' Making allowance for reminiscences of English spelling, and the accidents of type, this is an excellent specimen of the phases of English from German organs. It shows that sonants and surds do not always change place, as in *did, nobody, disturb, out, that, not,*

---

[1] Compare with a word in the following note sent to a druggist in Harrisburg, Pa. "Plihs lcht meh haf Sohm koh kohs Peryhs ohr Sähmting darhts guht vohr Ah lihttel Dahg Gaht lausse vor meh." [*Louse* for *loose* is common in the north of England. Thus in Peacock's Lonsdale Glossary (published for the Philological Society, 1869) we find: "**Louse**, *adj*. (1) loose. O.N. *laus*, solutus. (2) Impure, disorderly.—*v.t.* to loose. "To *lowse* 'em out on t' common" = To let cattle go upon the common.—**To be at a louse-end**. To be in an unsettled, dissipated state.—**Lous-ith'-heft**, *n*. a disorderly person, a spendthrift."—*A. J. Ellis*.]

[2] The *two* shows that this is a plural. When recognised, it will be observed that the law of its formation is legitimate.

come, which are not necessarily turned into *tit, nopotty, tisdurp, oud, dad, nod, gum*.[1]

In the foregoing example, the final *t* of *went* (where some might have expected 'wend'), *dit* for 'did,' *hat* for 'had,' *streat, wornt* for 'warned,' *put, srout* for 'throwed,' and *subscript*,—is for Latin -AT-US, English *-ed*, and as this is *t* in German, it is retained by the language instinct, even when represented by 'd,' as in *gol-d*. Were there not something different from mere accident here, Grimm's Law would be a delusion. The *t* of *out, disturb*, and the first one in *street*, is due to the surd *s* beside it, or in the German *aus* and *straszc*.

In *the, de; then, den; wis; anneysing, nosing; srout*, the sonant *th* becomes *d* by glottōsis,[2] and the surd one *s* by otōsis, or *t* by glottosis also, and 'no*th*ing' is more likely to become no*ss*ing or no*tt*ing, than no*dd*ing—and English *z* is not known to many German dialects. On the other hand, *z* as the representative of sonant *th*, is legitimate in the broken English of a Frenchman.

The *p* of 'open' and the *g* of 'against' are influenced by the German forms *öffnen* and *gegen*.

In "I dit nothin out annezmore"—*any* is made plural, and 'did out' (for the previous 'put out') seems to be a reminiscence of the German *austhun*.

§ 2. *The Breitmann Ballads.*

In these ballads Mr. Leland has opened a new and an interesting field in literature which he has worked with great success, for previous writers wanted the definite, accurate knowledge which appears in every page of Hans Breitmann, and which distinguishes a fiction like the Lady of the Lake from a

---

[1] For the word 'twenty-five,' the speaking and singing machine of the German Faber said *tventy-fife*, in imitation of its fabricator, using *t* and *f* because they occur in the German word. Similarly, fcif for *five* appears in the following joke from an American German newspaper :—

"Ein Pennfylvanifch - Deutfcher hatte zwei Pferde verloren und fchickte folgende Annonce : Ei loft mein tu Horfes! Der wonne ift a Sarrelhors, langen Schwanzthäl, fchort abgekuthet, aber weederum ausgrown ; der annerwonn is bläcker, aber mit four weiht Fieht un en weifzen Strich in his Fähs. Hu will bring mein tu Horfes bäck to mi, will rczief feif Thalers reward."

[2] *Hald.* Analytic Orthography, § 294.

figment like Hiawatha. Here we have an attempt to represent the speech of a large class of Europèan[1] Germans who have acquired English imperfectly, and who must not be confounded with the Pennsylvania German, altho the language of the two may have many points in common.

Apart from their proper function, and under their present spelling, the Breitmann ballads have but little philologic value. Instead of being the representative of an average speech, they contain forms which can hardly occur, even when influenced by the perversity of intentional exaggeration, such as shbeed, shdare, shdory, ghosdt, exisdt, lefdt, quesdions, excepdion, and where the sonant *d* occurs beside the surd *sh*, *f*, and *t*, in the lines :—

'De dimes he cot oopsetted[1]	[1] oopsettet.
In shdeerin lefdt und righdt.[2]	[2] G. recht.
Vas ofdener[3] as de cleamin shdars[4]	[3] G. öfter. [4] shtarrss.
Dat shtud de shky[5] py[6] nighdt.'	[5] sky. [6] G. bei.

In these pages an *average* speech is assumed as the basis of comparison, and also the average German who does one thing or avoids another in language. In such examples of bad English, surd and sonant (*p,b ; t,d ; k,gay*) must be confused, and German words like 'mit' for *with*, and 'ding' (rather than 'ting' or 'sing') for *thing*, may be introduced at discretion, as in Mr. Leland's use of *ding, mit, blitzen, erstaun*ished (for *-isht*), *Himmel, shlog*, and others.

When German and English have the same phase, it should be preserved, *book* (G. *buch*) has a sonant initial and a surd final in both languages; a German therefore, who brings his habits of speech into English, will not be likely to call a book a *boog, poog*, or *pook;* and Mr. Leland's habits as a German

[1] This accent is not wanted for Englishmen of the present day. Noah Webster (Dissertations on tho English Language, Boston U.S. 1789, p. 118) says : "Our modern fashionable speakers accent *European* on the last syllable but one. This innovation has happened within a few years. . . . . Analogy requires *Euro'pean* and this is supported by as good authorities as the other." He adds in a footnote. "*Hymenean* and *hymeneal* are, by some writers, accented on the last syllable but one ; but erroneously. Other authorities preserve tho analogy." Milton has *hymenéan*, P. L. 4, 711. Milton's line "Epicurean, and the Stoic severe," P. Reg. 4 280, is strange, however the word may be accented ; Shaksperc's "keep his brain fuming ; Épicurean cooks," A. and C., act 2, sc. 1, sp. 9, v. 24, is distinct enough. If the long diphthong or vowel in Latin were a proper guide, we should have to say *inimī'cal, doctrī'nal, amī'cable*. These words arc accented on the same plan as those taken from tho French. And this would give the common *Euro'pean*, which is now strictly tabooed.—*A. J. Ellis.*

scholar have led him to write *book, beer* (and *bier*) *fear, free,
drink, denn, trink, stately, plow, born, dokter, togeder, hart*
(hard), *heart, tead* (dead), *fought, frolic, goot, four, hat* (had,
hat,—but in the latter sense it should have been *het*), *toes,
dough* (though), *tousand, pills*, etc. Under this rule, his
'ploot' and 'blood' (G. blut) should have been *blut* :—

benny	*penny*	dwice	*tvice*	pefore	*before*	prown	*brown*
blace	*place*	fifdy	*fifty*	pegin	*begin*	py	*by*
blaster	*plaster*	giss	*kiss*	pehind	*behint*	prow	*brow*
breest	*priest*	led	*let*	plue	*blue*	scd	*to set*
creen	*green*	mighdy	*mighty*	pone	*bone*	streed	*shtreet*
deers	*tears*	pack n.	*back*	prave	*brafe*	veet	*feet*
dell	*tell*	pall	*båll*	pranty	*brandy*	vifdecn	*fifteen*
den	*ten*	peard	*beart*	preak	*break*	vine	*fine*
dwelve	*tvelf*	pecause	*becauss*	prings	*bringss*	wide	*vite*

In cases where the two languages do not agree in phase,
either phase may be taken, as in 'troo' or 'droo' for English
through with a surd initial, beside German *durch* with a
sonant; but as German cognate finals are more likely to be
surd than sonant (as in lock*wouth* for logwoo*d* at the end of
Ch. I. p. 6), *goot, hart* and *holt*, as breitmannish forms, are better
than *good, hard*, and *hold*. Mr. Leland practically admits
this, as in 'barrick' (G. *berg*, a hill), which, however, many
will take for a *barrack*.[1] The following have a different phase
in German and English—

day tay	door toor	-hood -hoot	red ret
diug ting	dream tream	hund- huntert	said set
dirsty tirsty	drop trop	middle mittle	saddle sattle
done tone	fader fater	pad path	drink trink

but *k*, and the pure final German *s* would turn *d* to *t* in
'bridges,' 'brackdise,' 'outsides,' 'holds,' 'shpirids;' it would
turn *g* to *k* in 'rags,' and it makes 'craps' (crabs) correct.
The power of English *z* can scarcely be said to belong to
average German, or to the breitmannish dialect; it should
therefore be *ss* in 'doozen,' 'preeze' (breeze), and 'phaze.'
When it is present it occurs initial, and we have 'too zee'
once, against numerous *s* initials like see, sea, say, so, soul, six.

The ballads have many irregularities in spelling like—as,
ash ; is, ish ; one, von ; two, dwo ; dwelf, dwelve, twelve,
zwölf (for tvelf) ; chor, gorus ; distants, tisaster ; dretful ;
tredful ; eck (the correct form), egg ; het, head, headt ;

---

[1] The probable breitmannish form of scythes is given in these pages. Compare "Pargerswill, Box [Parkersville, Bucks] Kaundie Pensilfäni."

groundt, cround, croundt ; land, lantlord, Marylandt; shpirid, shpirit, shbirit ; drumpet; trumpet ; foorst, foost, first, virst ; fein, vine; went, vent ; old, olt, oldt ; teufel, tyfel, tuyfel.

English *J* is placed in soobjectixe, objectified, jail, jammed, juice, jump (shoomp, choomp) ; it is represented by *sh* in shoost, shiant, shinglin ; by *ch* (correctly) in choin, choy, choke, enchine ; by *g*, *dg* in change, hedge ; and by *y* in Yane and soobjectifly—which is not objectionable. English *Ch* remains in catch, child, chaps (and shaps), fetch, sooch, mooch ; and it becomes *sh* in soosh (such), shase, sheek.

English *Sh* is proper in shmoke, shmile, shplit, shpill, shpoons, shtart, shtick, shtrike, shtop, shvear ; it is omitted in smack, stamp, slept ; and it is of doubtful propriety in ash (as), ashk, vash (was), elshe, shkorn, shkare, shky.

English *D* final is often written *dt* that the word may be recognised and the sound of *t* secured, as in laidt, roadt, shouldt, vouldt, findt, foundt, roundt (and round), vordt (and vord), obercoadt. English *ed* and its equivalents should be *et* or *t* in broken English, as in loadet, reconet, pe-markt, riset, signet, rollet, seemet, slightet, declaret, paddlet, mate (made), kilt ; *-ed* being wrong, as in said, coomed, bassed, scared, trinked, smashed, rooshed, bleased.

English *F*, *V*, *W*, receive the worst treatment, and are judged by the eye rather than by speech. German *folgen* and English *follow* are turned into 'vollow'; German *weil* is 'vhile' and 'while.' Other examples are wind and vindow ; vhen, vhene*f*er (turning not only German *v*, but English *v* into *f*), fery for *very*,—but svitch, ve (we), veight, vink, are proper. The following example is from 'Schnitzerl's Philosopede'—

'Oh vot ish all [1] dis eartly pliss ?	[1] *ol* in *folly*.
Oh, vot ish [4] man's soocksess ? [2]	[2] soocccess.
Oh, vot is various kinds [3] of dings ?	[3] *s* turns *d* into *t*.
Und vot is [4] hoppiness ?	[4] *iss* or *ish*, not both.
Ve find a pank node in de shtreedt,[5]	[5] shtreet.
Next[-sht] [6]dings [6] der pank ish [7] preak !	[6] dingss. [7] *d* requires *b*.
Ve folls [1] und knocks our outsides [8] in,	[8] G. *seit*, and final *s*,
Ven ve a ten-shtrike make.'	require *t*.

Chickis, near Columbia, Pennsylvania,
Feb. 16, 1870.

TRÜBNER & CO.'S PUBLICATIONS.

A DICTIONARY OF ENGLISH ETYMOLOGY.

By HENSLEIGH WEDGWOOD.

Second Edition, thoroughly revised and corrected by the Author, and extended to the Classical Roots of the Language. With an Introduction on the Formation of the Language. Imperial 8vo. pp. lxxii. and 744, double columns, cloth. 26*s.*

AMERICANISMS: THE ENGLISH OF THE NEW WORLD.

By M. SCHELE DE VERE, LLD.,

Professor of Modern Languages in the Univ. of Virginia. 8vo. pp. 685, cloth. 12*s.*

STUDIES IN ENGLISH:

OR, GLIMPSES OF THE INNER LIFE OF OUR LANGUAGE.

By M. SCHELE DE VERE, LL.D., Professor of Modern Languages in the University of Virginia. 8vo. cloth, pp. vi. and 365. 10*s.* 6*d.*

A DICTIONARY OF THE OLD ENGLISH LANGUAGE.

Compiled from Writings of the XII., XIII., XIV., and XV. Centuries. By FRANCIS HENRY STRATMANN. Second Edition. 4to. Part I. pp. 160. 10*s.* 6*d.* Part II. pp. 160. 10*s.* 6*d.*

THE WORKS OF WILLIAM SHAKESPEARE.

Edited according to the first printed copies, with the various readings, and Critical Notes, by F. H. STRATMANN. I. The Tragicall Historie of Hamlet, Prince of Denmarke. Demy 8vo., pp. vi. and 120, sewed. 3*s.* 6*d.*

AN OLD ENGLISH POEM OF THE OWL AND THE NIGHTINGALE.

Edited by F. H. STRATMANN. 8vo. cloth, pp. 60. 3*s.*

LANGUAGE AND THE STUDY OF LANGUAGE.

Twelve Lectures on the Principles of Linguistic Science. By WM. DWIGHT WHITNEY, Professor of Sanskrit, etc., in Yale College. Second Edition, augmented by an Analysis. Crown 8vo., cloth, pp. xii. and 504. 10*s.* 6*d.*

THE HOMES OF OTHER DAYS.

A History of Domestic Manners and Sentiments during the Middle Ages. By THOMAS WRIGHT, Esq., M.A., F.S.A. With illustrations from the Illuminations in Contemporary Manuscripts and other Sources. Drawn and engraved by F. W. Fairholt, Esq., F.S.A. One vol., medium 8vo., 350 Woodcuts, pp. xv. and 512, handsomely bound in cloth. 1*l.* 1*s.*

VOLUME OF VOCABULARIES,

Illustrating the Condition and Manners of our Forefathers, as well as the History of the forms of Elementary Education, and of the Languages Spoken in this Island, from the Tenth Century to the Fifteenth. Edited by THOMAS WRIGHT, Esq., M.A., F.S.A., etc., etc. [*In the Press.*]

THE CELT, THE ROMAN, AND THE SAXON.

A History of the Early Inhabitants of Britain down to the Conversion of the Anglo-Saxons to Christianity. Illustrated by the Ancient Remains brought to Light by Recent Research. By THOMAS WRIGHT, Esq., M.A., F.S.A., etc., etc. Third Corrected and Enlarged Edition. [*In the Press.*]

LONDON : TRÜBNER & Co., 8 AND 60, PATERNOSTER ROW.

www.ingramcontent.com/pod-product-compliance
Lightning Source LLC
Chambersburg PA
CBHW021524270326
41930CB00008B/1076